LETTERS TO ISABELLA STEWART GARDNER

HENRY JAMES

EDITED BY
ROSELLA MAMOLI ZORZI

PUSHKIN PRE

Pushkin Press
Somerset House, Strand
London WC2R 1LA

Text of Henry James's letters
Courtesy of Isabella Stewart Gardner Museum Boston

Introduction © Rosella Mamoli Zorzi, 2009
'Henry James, Mrs Gardner and Art' © Alan Chong, 2009

Pushkin Press first published *Letters to Isabella Stewart Gardner* in 2009

This edition first published in 2024

1 3 5 7 9 8 6 4 2

ISBN 13: 978-1-80533-091-2

All rights reserved. No part of this publication may be reproduced, stored in a retrieval system or transmitted in any form or by any means, electronic, mechanical, photocopying, recording or otherwise, without prior permission in writing from Pushkin Press

Cover: *Isabella Stewart Gardner in Venice*, 1894 by Anders Zorn

Offset by Tetragon, London
Printed and bound in the United Kingdom by Clays Ltd, Elcograf S.p.A.

www.pushkinpress.com

PUSHKIN PRESS CLASSICS

LETTERS TO ISABELLA STEWART GARDNER

'Such gossipy and effusive letters as these… let us see just why James was such a sought-after dinner-party guest'
THE INDEPENDENT

'The letters of Henry James… stand secure as one of the imaginative triumphs of the late nineteenth century'
LITERARY REVIEW

'The critical faculty hesitates before the magnitude of Mr Henry James's work. His books stand on my shelves in a place whose accessibility proclaims the habit of frequent communion'
JOSEPH CONRAD

HENRY JAMES was born in 1843 in New York City. One of the key figures of nineteenth-century literary realism, he wrote 20 novels, as well as numerous short stories, plays and books of criticism and travel writing. He is renowned for his work portraying the encounter of Americans with Europe. *The Portrait of a Lady* and *The Ambassadors* are amongst his masterpieces.

ROSELLA MAMOLI ZORZI is professor emerita of Anglo-American Literature at the University of Venice, Ca' Foscari. Her most recent work is the critical edition of *The Aspern Papers and Other Tales* by Henry James (Cambridge University Press, 2022), edited with Simone Francescater.

LETTERS TO ISABELLA STEWART GARDNER

CONTENTS

INTRODUCTION

It is quite astonishing that in the gold mine of letters[1] written by American novelist Henry James (1843–1916), many of those he wrote to Isabella Stewart Gardner (1840–1924) should still be unpublished and uncollected.

This astonishment derives from the fame of the writer, but also from that of his addressee, Isabella Stewart Gardner, a very wealthy New Yorker, who married an equally wealthy Bostonian banker, John Lowell Gardner, Jr (1837–98), in 1860. She was the creator of one of the most important museums in the United States, Fenway Court, or the Isabella Stewart Gardner Museum, in Boston, which opened with a gala on 1st January 1903, and to the public on 23rd February.

Mrs Gardner, often judged in the Boston newspapers and in more conservative society as an eccentric figure—which she probably enjoyed being—letting all sorts of 'legends' grow around her,[2] was surrounded by a 'court' of musicians, painters, novelists who revered and flattered her. John Singer Sargent caught the aura of her great power in his famous portrait of 1888, where Mrs Gardner, in a long black dress by the famous Paris couturier Worth, is shown exhibiting the signs of her wealth—she wears the purest pearls around her neck and waist, rubies attached to the pearls, and rubies glitter also on her black silk slippers. The motif of the golden background seems to crown her within a sort of holy nimbus, symbol of power, while her beautiful white neck and arms underline her feminine attractiveness.[3] In another famous portrait, of 1894, the Swedish painter Anders Zorn caught her extraordinary vitality, painting her as she stepped into the salon of the Palazzo Barbaro, the magnificent Venetian palace which Mrs Gardner rented more than once from its owners, Daniel and Ariana Curtis, while the moonlight shines in the background over the Grand Canal, and her open arms and hands are reflected in the window panes. The Venetian setting is highly significant, as the Barbaro was certainly an important inspiration for Isabella's Fenway Court—her lasting creation—where the simple exterior of the building hides a Venetian courtyard, where Gothic windows, partly original ones, look out into a space rich in Roman mosaics, sculptures, statues[4] and flowers.

"Dearest Queen", "*Chère charmeuse*", "Dear signora Isabella donna", "Dear Queen Isabella",[5] are some of the different ways in which friends of both sexes addressed Mrs Gardner in their letters, in adoring tones of absolute admiration. Isabella was respected, admired and flattered in her different decisions and actions, just like a queen.

Henry James's letters to her are different—they are full of admiration, but they manage to keep a distance, to proclaim the writer's independence in saving his precious time from too imposing and pressing invitations.[6] James's affection and esteem for Mrs Gardner are sincere and intense and become stronger and stronger as the years go by; the novelist recognizes openly Mrs Gardner's vitality and power, but he does not obey possible 'orders', even if this can be seen as a lack of faithfulness in their friendship: what is most important for James, in spite of his, at times, hectic social life, is the possibility of having time to devote to his writing, the real 'felicity' of his life.

In the spring of 1884, Mrs Gardner is approaching Europe and Venice by way of the Suez Canal after a one-year voyage around the world—the Gardners left Boston on 21st May 1883, and crossed the continent to San Francisco, from which they sailed aboard the *City of Tokio* on 29th May, to Japan, China, Cambodia, Java, India, and, via Aden and Cairo, to Crete, Zante, and finally Brindisi and Venice.[7] She expects to find James in Venice in May 1884, having written to him from Agra, the seat of the splendid Taj Majal, but her correspondent writes to her that he will not be there (letter 27). After almost throwing at her face her great power—"You have everything, you do everything, you enjoy everything"—James admits to broken vows, smashed promises, necessary, however, to save something even more valuable than friendship—his own writing. He declares that he knows too well she will not miss him, in her "preposterously pleasant career", and presents himself with the image of the "poor patient beast", developing to its utmost this metaphor and contrasting his own life of hard work with that of the lady travelling from the temples of Kyoto to Shanghai, from *La Sonnambula* in Java to the mountains of Shimla, enjoying life. But he will not join the crowd in spoiling her, as he is a real friend.

A tender irony allows James to save himself from becoming one of Mrs Gardner's courtiers, even if he enjoys a very intense relationship with her, as demonstrated by how often he sent her his books, on one occasion asking her to correct some misprints in one of his essays (letter 23), and by writing to her about his plays (letters 13–16, 21–22, 49) which he vainly hoped would make him as famous as his contemporary Oscar Wilde.

Mrs Gardner loves going to the theatre just as James loves the stage as a place of possible success—they go to the theatre together or James gives advice on something he saw, in particular the plays performed in Boston in 1883 by the Italian actor Salvini, about whose performance in *Othello* James is quite enthusiastic, even if he finds it odd that audiences should accept Shakespeare spoken in Italian by the great star, and in English by the rest of the company.[8]

The world encompassed in these letters is vast, in space and time. It includes two continents, Europe and America, since Mrs Gardner and James see each other on both sides of the Atlantic and correspond across its waters; but it also includes the Far East, where Mrs Gardner is traveling in 1883–84, and where other friends of both Mrs Gardner's and James's are, such as Percy Lowell or William Sturgis Bigelow; India, which the Gardners visit from north to south and where the Curtises announce they will go (letter 49); the West Indies and the South Sea islands, where Charles Robarts has some official post (letter 33). Reading these letters one realizes how much, how often and how far James's circle and generation travelled. Even the Fiji islands were part of their routes, not only for Robert Louis Stevenson but also for Henry Adams. If British friends travel in the British Empire, American friends seem not to have forgotten the Pacific Ocean whaling routes of their New England forebears.

The letters cover a wide space in time—they span a period of more than thirty years, from 1879 to 1914, a period full of world events, some of which appear in the letters—the Cuban war of 1898 (letter 67), which is a subject amply treated in its menacing power by Henry in his correspondence with his brother William, the famous psychologist and philosopher; echoes of "economic & labour convulsions, rumours of revolution & war" (letter 98) in 1911, announcing the coal strikes of 1912, which left "a couple of million people" out of work, "a number that will be hugely swelled if it goes on much longer",[9] in James's words; there are no letters for 1900, therefore neither the death of Queen Victoria nor the Boer War, which "drags its daily gloom along"[10] in Henry James's letters to William and other friends, are present.

One letter shows clearly on which side James was in a case that inflamed public opinion, the famous Dreyfus affair, where the trial leading to the condemnation to forced labour in 1894 of a Jewish French officer charged with treason was re-opened thanks to a famous article by Emile Zola, *J'accuse*, in 1898 (letter 69).

Among the great events of the century there was the 1893 Chicago World Columbian Exposition, to which the Gardners were invited, having lent a painting, and where Mrs Gardner saw *The Omnibus*, a picture by Anders Zorn. She bought the painting, and later invited the Zorns to Palazzo Barbaro, where the Swedish painter created Isabella's wonderful portrait. James imagines Mrs Gardner going to the Exposition, with her own building, a "more barbarous Barbaro", all of her own, among the Federal and the State buildings (letter 56).

The last letter, dated 20th April 1914, closes the correspondence, leaving out the great tragedy that made "the whole country" "a huge workshop of war", a few months later, bringing a "tremendous strain".[11]

People and letters cross the ocean, Mrs Gardner and James see each other in London, in Paris, in Venice, but also on the other shore of the Atlantic, in the various homes of Mrs Gardner, at Beacon Street in Boston, at Beverly on the Massachusetts coast, at Green Hill, in Brookline, near Boston.

Several letters allow us to enter the intense and private world of the deepest family affections—James writes to Mrs Gardner a particularly intense and moving letter on the death of his mother (letter 12), other letters regard other family losses—the death of Alice (1848–92)—letter 50, James's sister who died of cancer after a lifetime of psychological invalidism, and of William (1842–1910)—letter 92—his closest brother.

To Mrs Gardner James writes with great sympathy and affection after the sudden death of her husband on 10th December 1898 (letter 68).

Other personal losses and private tragedies are not recorded or only hinted at: there is no word on the suicide of Mrs Gardner's nephew, Joe Gardner,[12] on 16th October 1886, while there is an obscure reference to the suicide of Edith Story Peruzzi's son Bindo[13] in 1907 (letter 88), both perhaps linked to the persecution of homosexuals in the late nineteenth and early twentieth century; there is no letter covering the period of Oscar Wilde's trial in April 1895, on which James wrote to his brother William: "You ask of Oscar Wilde. His fall is hideously tragic—& the squalid violence of it gives him an interest (of misery) that he never had for me—in any degree—before. Strange to say he may have a 'future'—of a sort—by reaction—when he comes out of prison—if he survives the horrible sentence of hard labour that he will probably get. His trial begins today—however—& it is too soon to say."[14] Other private tragedies are mentioned in the letters, such as the suicide of the common friend Ellen Hooper Gurney in 1887; if James's sister Alice's illness is mentioned (letters 45–47),[15] no hint appears of the alcoholism and psychological weakness of their younger brother Robertson, mentioned in letter 78.

Across these wide spaces and dramatic times a varied world of artists, writers, public figures, mutual friends crop up.

Amazingly few letters allude to the works of art bought by Mrs Gardner, and to her final creation, the museum.

The almost total lack of references to art and art collecting in these letters does not allow us to see what James thought of Mrs Gardner's collection or of her purchases. The exception is the multiple mention of Titian's *Rape of Europa*, which was offered to her by Bernard Berenson. James commented on Mrs Gardner's acquisition of this painting in the course of 1898, merging with some irony the image of the buyer with that of the mythical figure (letter 65: 'incredible woman!—I mean *both* of you'), asking for more pictures of the painting (letter 66), finally imagining that Europa's fluttering purple scarf could bandage successfully Mrs Gardner's hurt back (letter 67).

He did imagine Mrs Gardner returning from Europe to her museum-home, in 1899, thinking of her in her "pictured halls", and as a figure in a "*cinquecento* tapestry" (letter 75), mentioning then in another letter her "recent splendid history & accomplished glory" (letter 76).

However, there are no other references to art purchases in the letters to Mrs Gardner which have come down to us. We must look elsewhere to try and understand James's opinion on the pervasive passion for art collecting of which Mrs Gardner was such an important representative in a period which witnessed the creation of other great American collections, such as those of J Pierpont Morgan, the Havemeyers, Henry Clay Frick, the Cone sisters and many others.

James was distinctly aware of this imposing phenomenon, linked to the making of huge fortunes in the fields of coal, railways, steel, sugar, shares and banking—those of the so-called 'Robber Barons', linked to the influence of aestheticism in the USA and to the rising culture of consumerism as theorized by Theodor Veblen in his well-known *Theory of the Leisure Class* (1899). Several of James's works of fiction dealing with collectors and collecting show how aware James was of all this, from the early stories *Adina* and *The Last of the Valerii*, to *The Portrait of a Lady* (1881), with its great European houses and the characters of the collectors, to *The Spoils of Poynton* (1896), a novel based exclusively on the passion and danger of collecting, *The Golden Bowl* (1904), a late novel presenting an American collector, and *The Outcry* (1911), a novel reflecting the debate over the right of England to sell its masterpieces to America.

In James's fiction the image of the collector and the passion for collecting is never totally positive. Is James's silence on Mrs Gardner's passion for art a sign of a negative attitude? We must turn to other sources to find an answer.

An unequivocally negative comment is to be found in a letter to Charles Eliot Norton, written from Lamb House on 24th–28th November 1899:

I have presently to take on myself a care that may make you smile, nothing less than to proceed, a few moments hence, to

> *Dover, to meet our celebrated friend (I think she can't* not *be yours) Mrs. Jack Gardner, who arrives from Brussels,* charged with the spoils of the Flemish school.[16]

The choice of "spoils" for Mrs Gardner's acquisition of "all her Van Eycks and Rubenses" which James "must help her to disembark" and see through the customs at Dover, leaves no doubt on James's negative judgement: *The Spoils of Poynton* had been published three years earlier.

But no mention of Mrs Jack's "spoils" is present in the letter written by James to Mrs Jack about this very arrival.

James's negative view of art acquisitions across the Atlantic comes up with great force as early as 1876, a period in which James was writing 'art reports' for the *Atlantic Monthly* and a few other journals and newspapers. In an article published in the *New York Tribune* in January 1876, the novelist wrote a series of comments on *The American Purchase of Meissonnier's Friedland* by a New Yorker, Mr A T Stewart. In this article, James, the frequenter of museums and galleries, the lover of art, the writer influenced by British aestheticism, the novelist and short-story writer who used a high number of works of art in his works, showed that he was well aware of the power of the market that had developed in those years, and he used a metaphor that seems to hover over his subsequent literary production.

James wrote:

> *the picture [Meissonnier's* Friedland*] has been bought by Mr. A.T. Stewart of New York for the prodigious sum, as I see it, of 380,000 francs. The thing is exceedingly clever, but it strikes me as* the dearest piece of goods *I ever had the honour of contemplating.*[17]

> *One takes … an acute satisfaction in seeing America* stretch out her long arm and rake in, across the green cloth of the wide Atlantic, the highest prizes of the game of civilization.[18]
> [my emphasis]

If the statement seems an appreciation ("One takes … an acute satisfaction"), the metaphor that follows undermines the positive quality of the statement. James used the metaphor of a gambler, playing on a billiard table extending from America to Europe ("the green cloth of the wide Atlantic"), "rak[ing] in" the most precious products of civilization. The obtaining of these prizes seems to be the casual, unmerited result of a gambling game, not of work.

A well-known later comment in James's *Notebooks* on "The Americans looming up—dim, vast, portentous—in their millions—like gathering waves—the barbarians of the Roman Empire"[19] (15th July 1895), coming immediately after a reference to the "Age of Mrs Jack", seems to underline James's horror of the grabbing hands of the moneyed American collectors. Was this "age of Mrs Jack", of the Fricks, the Morgans, the Havemeyers buying Titian's *Europa*, Holbein's *Thomas More*, illuminated medieval manuscripts, dozens of French impressionists, was this age the age of the "Barbarians"?

None of these negative comments is echoed in James's final judgement on Mrs Gardner's museum, as expressed in *The American Scene* (1907), the book on America written after a European absence of twenty years.

> … *no impression of the new Boston can feel itself hang together without remembrance of what it owes to that rare exhibition of the living spirit lately achieved, in the interest of the fine arts, and of all that is noble in them, by the unaided and quite heroic genius of a private citizen. To attempt to tell the story of the wonderfully-gathered and splendidly-lodged Gardner Collection would be to displace a little the line that separates private from public property* …
>
> *It is in the presence of the results magnificently attained, the energy triumphant over everything, that one feels the fine old disinterested tradition of Boston least broken.*[20]

This comment comes at the end of a chapter devoted to Boston and the disappearance of the old Boston, both in terms of architecture (houses torn down) and inhabitants (replaced by the "alien", or immigrants, especially Italian), indicating the obliteration of history—and memory—that James found in Boston as in New York.

The "new" Boston, where everything was too big, too new, too destructive of the past, does have a great gem: the collection of Isabella Stewart Gardner, the collection of a New York lady elevated to the honorary rank of a Bostonian, to the "fine old disinterested tradition of Boston".

The achievement of one woman collector found its utmost celebration in the words of a writer who was one of the sharpest critics of his home country and of the tycoon-collectors of art of his times in his fictional works.

ROSELLA MAMOLI ZORZI

NOTES

1 The total number of extant letters by Henry James is 10,423; in spite of the different collections, starting with the four pioneering volumes edited by Leon Edel, only a fraction of this number has been published. The huge and wonderful project of *The Complete Letters of Henry James* has started with volumes I and II, 1855–1872, edited by Pierre A Walker and Greg W Zacharias Introduction by Alfred Habegger Lincoln University of Nebraska Press 2006. For the number of letters, see vol I p lxviii.

2 On the legends of Mrs Gardner going around with a lion on a leash and such like, see Shand-Tucci pp 25–27 and Chong *Gondola Days*.

3 On the portrait, painted in December 1887 and January 1888, at Mrs Gardner's 152 Beacon Street house, in nine sittings, see Ormond-Kilmurray *The Early Portraits* pp 209–11. For the late watercolours, *Mrs Gardner at Fenway Court* (probably 1903) and *Mrs Gardner in White* (1922), see Ormond-Kilmurray 2003 no 442 p 100 and no 586 pp 251–52. See also Bourget's description in *Outre-Mer* (1895) pp 147–48. On Sargent and James, see *Sargent's Venice.*

4 On the collections, see Goldfarb and *Eye of the Beholder.*

5 These expressions, for instance, were used by Ralph Curtis, painter, son of the owners of the Palazzo Barbaro in Venice, and Mrs Bronson, an American who lived in Venice and Asolo, and a friend of Robert Browning, who sent Mrs Gardner a lock of the poet's hair.

6 See also Edel *Conquest of London* p 380.

7 All references to Mr and Mrs Gardner's travels are based on their travel diaries and scrapbooks, courtesy of the Isabella Stewart Gardner Museum Boston. For excerpts of Mrs Gardner's letters from the Orient, see Carter pp 59–86.

8 *Scenic Art* p 170.

9 Letter to T S Perry of 21st March 1912 p 338.

10 *The Correspondence of William James, William and Henry* III p 101.

11 Letter to Thomas S Perry 15th January 1915 p 347.

12 See Shand-Tucci pp 82–84.

13 See Lawrence pp 1–20.

14 *The Correspondence of William James, William and Henry* II p 359 (letter of 26th April 1895, the day on which Wilde's trial began, finishing on 25th May, with the imprisonment of Wilde).

15 For Alice James, see Edel *Diary of Alice James*, and Strouse.

16 Edel *Letters IV* p 124.

17 *Painter's Eye* p 108.

18 Ibid p 108.

19 *Notebooks* p 126. For a wider analysis of James's *Notebooks* and letters with regard to collecting and Isabella Stewart Gardner, see my essay in *Power Underestimated: American Women Art Collectors* Proceedings of the International Conference organized by the Frick Collection and the University of Venice April 2008. On collecting, see also *Before Peggy Guggenheim*, Cagidemetrio, Francescato, Perosa.

20 *American Scene* p 255.

EDITOR'S NOTE

Of the hundred letters presented here, eighty-three have never been published in English (they were all published in my Italian translation for Archinto, in Milan, 2004). Of the seventeen previously published, more precisely: four letters (21, 55, 64, 98) were published by Percy Lubbock; ten (6, 10, 11, 12, 22, 23, 43, 49, 54, 74—this last one also by Morris Carter) by Leon Edel; three (27, 42, 59) by myself.

The indication 'Ms I S G M' below the letter number means 'Manuscript, Isabella Stewart Gardner Museum'; 'Lubbock', 'Edel' and 'Mamoli Zorzi' refer to the letters published by these editors (see Bibliography).

My transcriptions are those of the manuscripts (with the exception of two typed letters, dictated by James) preserved at the Isabella Stewart Gardner Museum in Boston. Transcriptions are as faithful as possible to the original letters: for example, dates are transcribed in the irregular ways James used; italics indicate words underlined once by James; words with one underlining were underlined twice, or three times, by James; abbreviations are kept the way James wrote them. However, no indication is given of deleted words in the letters.

I have been helped in deciphering some difficult words by Philip Horne, University College London, by Tamara Follini, Clare College Cambridge, and by Pierre Walker, Salem State College, whom I would like to thank for their repeated generosity in my work on Jamesian texts; Clara Kozol's transcriptions made for the Museum and her dating of some letters have been of great help, as has her essay *Henry James and Mrs Gardner: A New Perspective*, in *Fenway Court* Isabella Stewart Gardner Museum Boston 1973 pp 2–9. Of course any possible mistake in the transcriptions is mine.

Jack Gardner's unpublished diaries, Mrs Gardner's scrapbooks and guestbooks, held at the Museum, have been very useful.

ROSELLA MAMOLI ZORZI

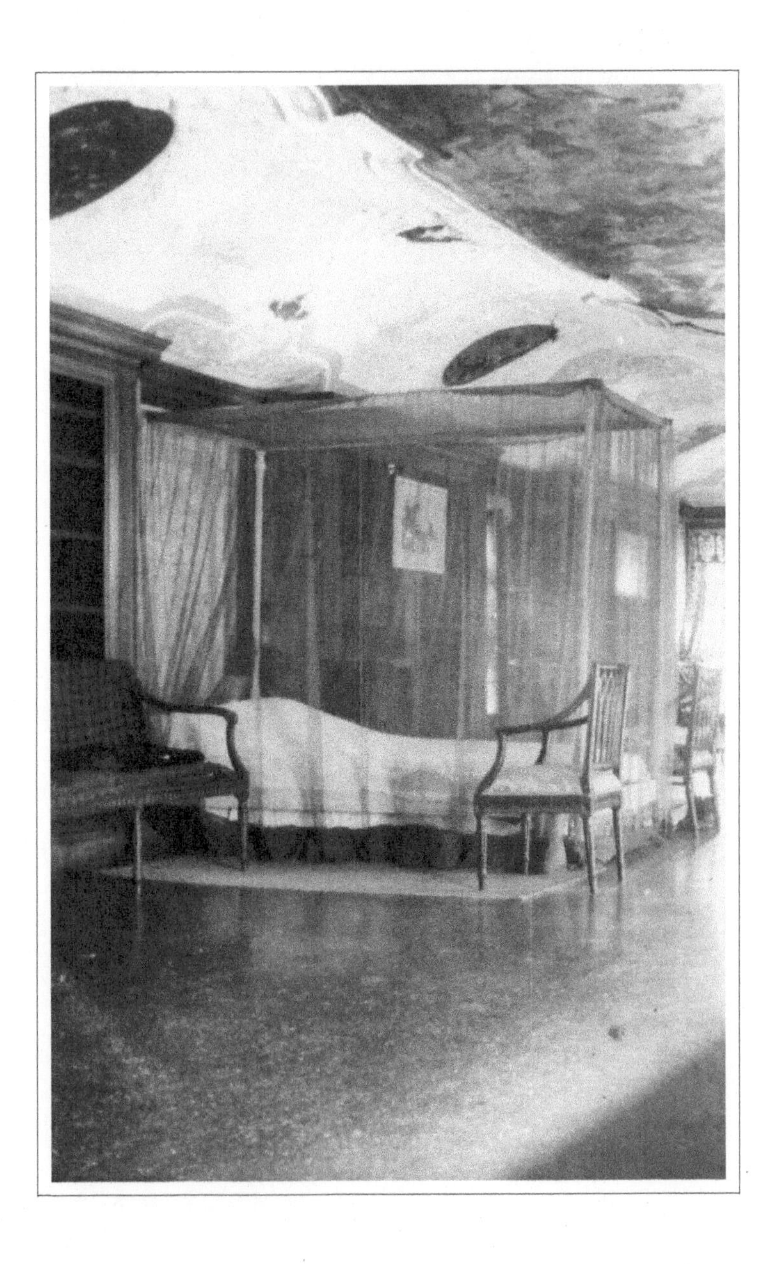

HENRY JAMES, MRS GARDNER AND ART

Henry James and Isabella Gardner were bound together in innumerable ways—by a shared social circle stretching from Boston to London and Venice, a love of theatre and music, an interest in gossip and a devotion to attractive young men.[1] And they were both devoted to Italy, Venice especially. But most profoundly, they both loved art. This passion is not well illuminated in their surviving correspondence, leaving us to speculate on their discussions and to consider their common modes of thinking, conducted in very different ways and often from afar.

In one of James's earliest letters to Gardner (2 of 1879), he provided her with the address of the painter Edward Burne-Jones and a recommendation: "his things are very interesting (*I* think, at least)". And in a review from about the same time, James singled out the artist for praise.[2] We do not know if Isabella actually visited the artist, but she bought nothing by him.

Indeed at this time, Isabella could hardly be called a collector at all. She owned, by this date, paintings by Charles-Émile Jacque and Narcisse-Virgile Diaz, and at this early period bought modest works from local Boston galleries—furnishings common in American upper-class residences.

Henry James, however, was intimately familiar with the contemporary art scene, in part through the many reviews he was writing in the 1870s. He played a crucial role in introducing Isabella to the lively world of art exhibitions in London and Paris in 1879 and through the 1880s. More important, James introduced Isabella to artists, and from this point in time, she surrounded herself with artists, socialized with them, befriended them and bought work directly from them. Indeed, James can be credited with initiating what would become an all-consuming passion for Isabella.

Burne-Jones's address was just one of many such introductions. An especially important event was a party at the Grosvenor Gallery on 21st July 1879, when Isabella first met James McNeill Whistler.[3] The gallery's third summer exhibition included works by Whistler. Henry James, Henry Adams, and Jack and Isabella all went to the reception.[4] In September of the same year James accompanied the Gardners to Paris.

Isabella and James had very different opinions of Whistler's work, one of many examples where their taste diverged. In 1878, James described the Ruskin-Whistler trial, and characterized Whistler's work: "Unfortunately, Mr. Whistler's productions are so very eccentric and imperfect (I speak here of his paintings only; his etchings are quite another affair, and altogether admirable) … "[5] Isabella was much more enthusiastic. In October 1886, she bought a small painting and two pastels, including a portrait of herself. In the 1890s, she acquired numerous etchings as well as two landscape paintings. In the mid-1890s there was even discussion of her acquiring Whistler's famous *Peacock Room* for the Boston Public Library, although nothing came of the idea.

Henry James's most significant act of mediation was introducing Isabella to John Sargent in 1886. Sargent's *Madame X* (Metropolitan Museum of Art) had taken Paris by storm, and James arranged a private viewing of the scandalous portrait in the privacy of the artist's studio (letter 31). Enthusiastic about Sargent's painting, James had quickly befriended the artist. In 1887, James published an insightful appraisal of Sargent's work in *Harper's Magazine* where he commented on *Madame X* as well as on paintings that had made their way to Boston, including the *Portrait of the Boit Children* (Museum of Fine Arts) and *El Jaleo* (now in the Gardner Museum).[6] Isabella would undoubtedly have met Sargent with or without James, especially since the artist came to Boston in

1887 to paint society portraits of many of Isabella's friends. But her enthusiasm was certainly stoked by James, who made sure that she was familiar with the range of Sargent's work. Indeed the novelist seems to have guided her approach to working artists. In Boston, Sargent painted a remarkable portrait of Mrs Gardner, but its unusual pose and background are as much her creation as his. She clearly desired a portrait that would make a splash—that would seem unique, if not actually as controversial as the sensuous display of flesh in *Madame X*. James described Sargent's portrait of Isabella without having seen it, calling it (appropriately) a "Byzantine Madonna with a halo".[7]

But even with Sargent, James and Gardner parted ways. *El Jaleo*, exhibited at the Salon of 1882, was not to James's liking:

> *It looks like life, but it looks also, to my view, rather like a perversion of life, and has the quality of an enormous 'note' or memorandum, rather than of a representation …* 'El Jaleo' *sins, in my opinion, in the direction of ugliness and, independently of the fact that the heroine is circling round incommoded by her petticoats, has a want of serenity.*[8]

Isabella could not have disagreed more. The painting had been purchased by a relative of Jack Gardner's, T Jefferson Coolidge, who brought it to Boston. Isabella craved it, apparently for decades; in 1914, she created an entire gallery to display *El Jaleo* in an evocative manner, and she succeeded in obtaining the painting as a gift.

Isabella Gardner in turn seems to have inspired Henry James—she can perhaps be glimpsed in various characters, although the connection is always obtuse and based on transformed details of personality and habit. James's notebooks explicitly record Isabella, not always in a flattering way. In 1895, struck by the "insane frenzy of futile occupation imposed by the London seasons", he imagined a character based on Isabella—"the age of Mrs Jack, the figure of Mrs Jack".[9] Did James associate Gardner with activity lacking serious thought? On other occasions James marvelled at her energy—in 1892 she acquired chairs from the Borghese collection: "The little lady is of an energy! She showed me yesterday at Carrer's her seven glorious chairs (the loveliest I ever saw); but they are not a symbol of her attitude—she never sits down."[10]

The same year in Venice, Gardner commissioned portraits of herself and Jack from the Viennese artist, Ludwig Passini. Katharine Bronson gave a large dinner party for the Gardners, and James had the opportunity to talk to Passini. The artist remarked that the Empress Frederick of Germany knew exactly how to pose for a portrait, and James conceived the idea that since aristocrats had posed for artists their entire lives, even deposed royalty would never lose that particular skill. The story has a cruel edge to it since Passini's portrait of Isabella is awkward in the extreme, and James must have been struck by Isabella's failure to pose well for a portrait. Passini's portrait does not survive and may have been destroyed by Isabella.[11]

James understood Isabella's desire to collect, and to create a public museum that would reflect her personality. Indeed, he seems to have come to this realization after spending extended periods with her at the Palazzo Barbaro in Venice. He wrote to her in 1893 (letter 56) saying that he imagined her at the Chicago World's Fair with her own building, "an infinitely more barbarous Barbaro—all to yourself … in a category by itself, Mrs Jack's building?" He wished for his own apartment at the top, like the bed he had in the Palazzo Barbaro's library.

This is a joke, of course, but a prophetic one. James had detected in Isabella's energy and ambition the possibility of some kind of Venetian construction devoted to art—a vision encouraged by her enthusiastic first steps as a collector.

Isabella and James did not see much of each other or correspond in the period when she was building and installing her new museum in Boston, so consumed was she with its preparation prior to its opening in January 1903. In 1904, James returned to America after an absence of twenty-one years, and saw Fenway Court for the first time.

James went on drives and spent time with Isabella at Green Hill, where he met her new friend Okakura Kakuzō, the author of *The Book of Tea*. In his notebook, he recalled his time "with Mrs Gardner (ah, to squeeze a little, a little of what I felt, out of that, too!) at Brookline, at her really so quite *picturable* Green Hill—which would yield a 'vignette,' I think, whereof I fully possess all the elements".[12]

In *The American Scene*, his look at his native country, published in 1907, James attempted to place Isabella's new museum within the Bostonian as well as American tradition of the arts. He applauded the "rare exhibition of the living spirit lately achieved, in the interest of the fine arts, and of all that is noblest in them, by the unaided and quite heroic genius of a private citizen". He meant, of course, Isabella, and he contrasted her efforts, somewhat surprisingly, with the aggressive philanthropy found in the foundation or expansion of universities, which constructed vast empty facilities waiting to be used. Rather, he celebrated Isabella's passionate love of art—and the idea of presenting it to the public:

> *To attempt to tell the story of the wonderfully-gathered and splendidly-lodged Gardner Collection would be to displace a little the line that separates private from public property; and yet to find no discreet word for it is to appear to fail of feeling for the complexity of conditions amid which so undaunted a devotion to a great idea (undaunted by the battle to fight, losing,*

> *alas, with State Protection of native art, and with other scarce less uncanny things) has been able consummately to flower. It is in presence of the results magnificently attained, the energy triumphant over everything, that one feels the fine old disinterested tradition of Boston least broken.*[13]

However, James says nothing about the particular character of the art and installation of Fenway Court. On a visit to the Museum of Fine Arts, then still at Copley Square (the new building would open in 1909), he was taken by a small sculpture of Aphrodite. So charged was this delicate work, that it seemed to change its surrounding, even to "make a garden".

> *I felt this quarter of the Boston Art Museum bloom, under the indescribable dim eyes, with delicate flowers. The impression swallowed up every other; the place, whatever it was, was supremely justified, and I was left cold by learning that a much bigger and grander and richer place is presently to overtop it.*[14]

James also noted that objects of importance were usually condemned to cold and antiseptic surroundings: "Objects doomed to distinction make round them a desert". Isabella's museum, like portions of the old Museum of Fine Arts, was an antidote to this approach. James instinctively shared with Isabella an understanding that art needed to be seen in a rich setting. He had seen the cold new facilities of the universities and feared the construction of the new Museum of Fine Arts building. It therefore seems that ancient Aphrodite in the Museum of Fine Arts is actually a surrogate for Isabella Gardner's museum, in particular as he imagines a garden around the sculpture. In fact, at the heart of Fenway Court lay a real garden adorned with ancient sculpture.

Isabella never spelt out her museological philosophy, but her circle of friends formulated many of its principles. Matthew Prichard, the assistant to the director of the Museum of Fine Arts, and a close friend of Isabella's, tried to explain the unique environment of Fenway Court. In an essay of 1911, he attempted to describe the evocative powers of the place:

> *You visit a lady of feeling. She receives you in a room hung with tapestry; someone is playing on the piano; your friend is charmingly dressed and she wears jewellery; there are flowers about. You sit down and talk with her ... you were aware of the various elements affecting you during the call, the music, the flowers, the dress and so on, but you did not examine them ... you did not conceptualize them. It appeared all as one harmony ... Do you not think that such an experience may be typical of what we call art?*[15]

In this view, the Gardner Museum's multisensory experience prevented visitors from analysing individual objects in an intellectual fashion. This is remarkably close to James's contrast of two modes of looking—he starts as the "restless analyst" but gives way to the emotion of the "sonneteer".[16] Prichard and others in Isabella's circle such as the painter John La Farge also attacked an overly analytical and academic approach to art. La Farge likened her museum to poetry: its collection "is but the necessary filling in of a manner of poem, woven into the shape of a house by a mind recalling likings and the memories of the past, and so much of a creation that the mistress' own hand has mixed the very tones that colour the walls, chamfered the beams of the ceilings, as well as planned the scheme and disposal of the entire building".[17]

Isabella Gardner purposefully avoided interpretive or philosophical statements, which suggests that she regarded the meaning of Fenway Court as unfixed. The personal combinations of paintings, furniture and sculpture might evoke particular meanings and associations, but the visitor is entirely free to experience art emotionally and to construct meanings indirectly. This absence of a single authoritative reading can be likened to the shifting points of view encountered in James's late novels. As Isabella was conceiving her museum in the period 1899 to 1902, James was developing an innovative narrative technique that allowed the reader to follow the thoughts of various characters in succession. For example, events in *The Wings of the Dove*, published in 1902, unfold from the point of view of several different individuals.

In the novel, Milly Theale, a dying young American heiress, rents an art-filled palace on the Grand Canal in Venice in which to spend her final days, sheltered from the quotidian world. James himself said that Milly was partly based on his beloved cousin Minny Temple, who had died from tuberculosis, but the character also resembles Isabella Gardner. Both always wore long strings of pearls and, more significant, like Milly Theale, Isabella regularly rented a palace in Venice—the Palazzo Barbaro, which inspired both her and James.

> *Hung about with pictures and relics, the rich revered and served … Milly moved slowly to and fro as the priestess of the worship. Certainly it came from the sweet taste of solitude, caught again and cherished for the hour; always a need of her nature, moreover, when things spoke to her with penetration. It was mostly in stillness they spoke to her best; amid voices she lost the sense.*[18]

There is no doubt that the setting for *The Wings of the Dove* was the Palazzo Barbaro, since its owners were described as a kindly American couple—in real life, Daniel and Ariana Curtis. And for the New York Edition of his oeuvre, James sent Alvin Coburn to photograph the palazzo for the frontispiece. But more important, James characterized the novel's palace as an ideal museum—when bad weather forced Merton

Densher to remain in the palace, the day "had passed for him like a series of hours in a museum, though without the fatigue of that; and it had also resembled something that he was still, with a stirred imagination, to find a name for".[19]

Henry James's brother, William, was bothered by the shifting perspective and willful obscurity of *The Wings of the Dove.* He complained to the novelist: "You've reversed every traditional canon of story-telling (especially the fundamental one of telling the story, wh. you carefully avoid)."[20] This narrative imprecision—"the complication of innuendo and associative reference"[21]—characterizes both the novel and Isabella Gardner's palace. Crucial conversations and plot developments are only hinted at in the novel, a practice paralleled in Gardner's suggestive, non-expository museum. Both novel and museum entice their audiences into creating their own readings.

The palace in *The Wings of the Dove* functions as an escape from time, from the frivolous and commercial world, but also, for Milly Theale, from death. Like Fenway Court, the structure is filled with beautiful objects and seems to belong to no particular point in time. James wrote: "she insisted that her palace—with all its romance and art and history—had set up round her a whirlwind of suggestion that never dropped for an hour. It wasn't therefore, within such walls, confinement, it was the freedom of all the centuries."[22]

The poetic imprecision of this language—romance and suggestion, art and history—is far removed from that of the critic or the art historian, but much closer to the spirit of Fenway Court, especially as articulated by Prichard and La Farge. Henry James and Isabella Gardner worked in parallel, sharing an approach, and dipping into the common repository of ideas. Like James, Isabella left her audience with a variety of narrative possibilities and sensory experiences, rather than specific encodings of meaning. Often caricatured as embodiments of a tradition-bound, Old World elite, Isabella Gardner and Henry James, in their respective fields, now seem surprisingly modern.

ALAN CHONG

NOTES

1 Henry James *Beloved Boy*; *Dearly Beloved Friends*.

2 *Nation* 29th May 1879; *The Painter's Eye* p 182.

3 Mrs Henry Adams to her father 21st July 1879; Richard Lingner in *Eye of the Beholder* p 196.

4 Anne Procter wrote on 31st July 1879: "Then on one Monday Eve: as all went in our best frocks and I never saw a prettier party—the dark red walls made a good background—and the famous beauties looked better than usual." Correspondence of James McNeill Whistler: www.whistler.arts.gla.ac.uk.

5 *Nation* 19th December 1878; *Painter's Eye* p 174.

6 Henry James 'John S Sargent' *Harper's Magazine* 75 1887 pp 683–91. Revised version in *Painter's Eye* pp 216–228.

7 James based his comment on Lady Playfair's description of it. James to Miss Reubell 22nd February 1888; Ormond-Kilmurray *The Early Portraits* p 210.

8 James 'John S Sargent' pp 686, 688.

9 *Notebooks* p 126.

10 James to Ariana Curtis 10th July 1892; *Letters from the Palazzo Barbaro* p 122.

11 Chong *Gondola Days* pp 99–100: with illustrations of Passini's portraits of the Empress Frederick and Isabella Gardner.

12 *Notebooks* p 126. Adeline Tintner 1993 p 153, incorrectly says Isabella's painting by Vermeer, among others, was at Green Hill (which explains the word '*picturable*'); however, Isabella's collection had been at Fenway Court since 1902.

13 Henry James *The American Scene* edited by John F Sears Harmondsworth 1994 pp 188–89.

14 Ibid pp 187–88.

15 Typescript in ISGM; dated 11th–24th March 1911 (Paris) p 2; addressed to Denman Ross. Discussed in Alan Chong, 'Mrs. Gardner's Museum of Myth,' RES, no. 52 (Autumn 2007).

16 *American Scene* p 187.

17 John La Farge *Noteworthy Paintings in American Private Collections* edited by J La Farge and A Jaccaci New York Jaccaci 1907 vol 1 p 3.

18 Henry James *The Wings of the Dove: A Norton Critical Edition* edited by J Donald Crowley and Richard A Hocks New York Norton 1978 p 337.

19 Ibid p 360.

20 William James to Henry James 25th October 1902; *The Correspondence of William James* vol 3 p 220. William Dean Howells described the novel in similar terms; for this and other commentary, see *The Wings of the Dove* cit.

21 William James to Henry James 4th May 1907; *Correspondence of William James* p 338.

22 *The Wings of the Dove* cit p 361.

LETTERS BY HENRY JAMES

I

(Ms I S G M)

3, Bolton Street,
Piccadilly. W *Friday* 13*th* June [1879]

Dear Mrs. Gardner
I have just been giving away a couple of places[1] which I myself had taken for Wednesday 18*th*, owing to a pressing engagement which promised to make it impossible I shd. use them. But on Monday 23*d* I shall be very happy, & will come & dine with you with pleasure at 6.30, sharp. With very good wishes for your prosperity meanwhile, very truly yours

H. James jr

The name of the Photographer shop in South Audley St. (quite the best) is *Macmichael's*. I forget the number, but it is the last shop on the right, just before Grosvenor Square.—

NOTE

1 James frequented and loved the London theatres, and he wrote several essays on the London plays of that period, expressing, however, highly critical opinions on fashionable theatre-going. His first essay, *The London Theatres*, was finished in May 1878; his second, *The Comédie Française*, about the company's highly successful six weeks in London, was completed on 12th July 1879; a third essay, *The London Theatres—1880*, was published in January 1881. See *Scenic Art*. On 18th June 1879, there were about two dozen London theatres with performances going on: among them, at the Royal Italian Opera, Covent Garden, Adelina Patti sang in *Trovatore*; at the Princess's Theatre *Drink* offered a stage version of Zola's *L'Assommoir*; at the Lyceum there was a *Hamlet* (with Henry Irving and Ellen Terry); the Comédie Française was performing Marivaux's *Le jeu de l'amour et du hazard*. James wrote on Henry Irving and his *Hamlet* (*Scenic Art* pp 122, 138) and went to the Comédie Française in London several times, writing about it, as mentioned above, and he also wrote about Charles Warner, "who for unnumbered months distinguished himself as the Anglicized hero of the dramatization of Emile Zola's *L'Assommoir*".

II

(Ms I S G M)

3, Bolton Street,[1]
Piccadilly.W

July 5th [1879]

Dear Mrs. Gardner
I hasten to transcribe B.J's address-[2]

E. Burne Jones esq.
The Grange
North End Road
Fulham.

—It is rather far away—beyond South Kensington—a house in which old Richardson,[3] the author of "Clarissa Harlowe" lived—but his things are very interesting (*I* think, at least;) and you are perfectly free to present yourself & ask to see them. There is usually indeed a number of people doing the same.—I greatly wish I were at liberty to go with you, but tomorrow p.m. I am doubly, trebly engaged. This is my chronic condition just now, but I am looking forward to greater freedom a week hence, & to the prospect then of being able—if you will allow me—to see you oftener. I cherish this hope. It is very kind of you to go on liking London—if you do!—with these detestable days.[4] With very good wishes, very truly—

H. James jr

NOTES

1 From the autumn of 1876 James lived at this address for ten years, having decided to stay in Europe and in London.

2 Edward Burne-Jones (1833–98), the well-known British Pre-Raphaelite painter, whose studio—The Grange—James frequented until the painter's death. James wrote more than once appreciatively on Burne-Jones, usually in connection with his exhibitions at the Grosvenor Gallery: in 1877 on his *Venus's Mirror* and *Days of Creation*, in 1878 on his *Laus Veneris* and *Chant d'Amour*, in 1879 on his *Annunciation* and four other pictures (see *Painter's Eye*). The London Grosvenor Gallery (see letter 6), founded by Lady Lindsay and her husband Sir Coutts Lindsay of Belcarres (1824–1913), represented an innovative venue opposed to the more conservative Royal Academy; it was open from 1877 to 1890, and exhibited important artists such as Whistler, whose famous trial against Ruskin was caused by an insulting sentence said there; many women artists, including the Montalbas, were also welcome there. In 1902 James published a story, *Flickerbridge*, which may have been inspired by the series of Burne-Jones's paintings *Briar Rose* (1870–90), for the metaphors about *Sleeping Beauty*, as A Tintner suggests (Tintner 1986 pp 17–23). Mrs Gardner does not seem to have ever bought paintings by Burne-Jones: two drawings by him for a stained-glass window were offered to her by Charles Eliot Norton in 1903, but she did not buy them (McCauley *Gondola Days* p 39).

3 The British novelist Samuel Richardson (1689–1761), author of the well-known epistolary novels *Pamela* (1740–41) and *Clarissa Harlowe* (1747–48), which James knew quite well and quoted several times in his essays.

4 On 8th June of that year James wrote about the horrible weather to Grace Norton, lamenting "the dark and dreadful winter", "the most ingeniously detestable one I have ever known" (Edel *Letters II* p 239); on 6th July James wrote to his mother, again lamenting the "incessant rain and the darkest dismallest cold" (ibid p 247). In his essays on London, there are innumerable references to the sootiness, blackness and murkiness of the city, which are always balanced by James's love for its life and liveliness. In this period John Ruskin, starting from the bad weather and the black clouds full of rain and also surely of factory soot, elaborated the theories expressed in his lectures, *The Storm-Cloud of the Nineteenth Century*, given in 1884, in which the meteorological clouds became symbolic of the moral decline of British society.

III

(Ms I S G M)

3, Bolton Street,
Piccadilly. W

July 15th [1879][1]

Dear Mrs. Gardner
If I hear nothing from you to the contrary I shall present myself at dinner on Friday next—& shall assume 7.45 to be your hour. I have just heard from the housekeeper at Hatfield,[2] who puts us off to next week, as the Family (with a very big capital) are to be there in the interval. On Friday, then, I shall propose the following *Wednesday* or Thursday. Your appreciation of this dear old London under these persistently inhuman skies is one of the most magnanimous things I know! With kindest regards to your gentlemen[3]—yours very faithfully

H. James jr

NOTES

1 The date is at the end of the letter.

2 Hatfield House, in Hertfortshire, the magnificent dwelling of the Marquess of Salisbury. It was built in 1611 by Robert Cecil (1563–1612), 1st Earl of Salisbury and chief minister to King James I. It is well known for its rich and precious interior, paintings and furniture, and for its park, designed by John Tradescant at the beginning of the seventeenth century. The place also included the 'Old Palace', or former Royal Palace (c 1485), where Queen Elizabeth I spent much of her childhood. The 'Family' at that time was represented by Robert Cecil, 3rd Marquess of Salisbury (1830–1903), who was Foreign Secretary in 1878, after having been Secretary for India (1866–67 and 1874–76). He then became Prime Minister (1885–86, 1886–92, 1895–1902). Not only was the 'Family' there, but there were over a hundred guests on the Saturday, from three to seven o'clock, including the Prince and Princess of Wales, the Crown Prince of Sweden and Norway, the hereditary Grand Duke of Baden and other royal guests and ambassadors. A dinner for the 'house party' of forty was served in the evening in the Marble Hall, as *The Times* of 21st July reported. There seems to be no record of James's and Mrs Gardner's visit, but we know the name of the housekeeper who postponed James's visit: Catherine Orme, born in Bedford c 1813, as kindly communicated to me by Victoria Perry, of Hatfield House.

3 James sends his regards to Mr John Gardner (called Jack), and to his orphaned nephews, William Amory and Augustus Gardner, who were taken by Isabella and John Gardner to

Europe for a grand tour in 1879. The Gardners looked after them and their brother, Joseph (Joe), with great affection, but on 16th October 1886, Joe committed suicide, like his father, John Gardner's brother, Joseph (b 1827), who had killed himself on 12th June 1875. See McCauley *Gondola Days* p 5. For an analysis of the homosexual milieu and the possible causes of Joe's suicide and Mrs Gardner's eventually accepting attitude, see Shand-Tucci p 84.

IV

(Ms I S G M)

Reform Club.
Pall Mall. S.W *July 22^{d}* [1879]

Dear Mrs. Gardner-

The weather doesn't seem to be mending, but I should say that we had better assume that we shall go to Hatfield to morrow (Wednesday) morning. There is a good train at 12 o'clock from King's Cross which takes us there in 35 minutes, & there are plenty of trains to come back by: the *3.6*, or *4.45* being, I shld. suppose, the best. It is a longish drive to King's X & I will come in tomorrow at 11:15. to converse with you & start at the same time. I hope you will bring those brilliant boys![1]—I hope too you were none the worse for last night[2] & didn't dream of Mrs Walter Crane![3] A' demain- yours ever

H. James jr

NOTES

1 Mr Gardner's nephews, see letter 3, note 3.

2 Apparently the evening of Monday 21st July, when James and Mrs Gardner went to the Grosvenor Gallery, as Mrs Adams writes in a letter to her father. After a dinner for eight, at ten o'clock "went to a party at the Grosvenor Gallery. Many people one was glad to see … Mrs Jack Gardner was there, and we had some twenty minutes side by side in the vestibule waiting for our respective broughams, and sympathysed over the awful gowns. Down come an elderly female in black, followed by a jolly looking very fat one, and the Britons fall back on either side and bend their sovereign-loving knees, because it's the Grand Duchess of Mecklenburg-something and her sister Mary of Teck. Mrs Gardner and I smile pityingly on the Britons" (*Letters of Mrs Henry Adams* p 159). Princess Augusta of Cambridge (1822–1916), Duchess of Mecklenburg-Strelitz, aunt of Queen Mary, wife of George V. For the Adamses, see letter 6, note 3.

3 Mary Crane, the wife of British painter and Tennyson's and children's books illustrator Walter Crane (1845–1915), who exhibited at the Grosvenor Gallery. Why she should influence the dreams of Mrs Gardner has not been identified. There does not seem to have been an upsetting or terrifying picture by Walter Crane at the Grosvenor Gallery Summer Exhibition for 1879; see *Grosvenor Notes, with Facsimiles of Sketches by the Artists* edited by Henry Blackburn London Chatto and Windus May 1879 vol I.

V

(Ms I S G M)

42 Rue Cambon[1] [15–22 September 1879]

My dear Mrs. Gardner
It is delightfully kind of you to propose my going to Rheims[2]—but I really can't. I write this line, instead of going to see you, because I have (in the first place) a long list of duties for this p.m.; & (in the 2^d place,) feel so sad & bitter about not being able to respond to your suggestion, that I shld. break down if I attempted to talk to you about it—make a scene, shed tears &c. I *can't* go—I have still a *density* of occupation here. I don't believe, for that matter, that *you* will go to Rheims yourself, as it is by no means on the way to Boulogne.—Thank you, tenderly, for this & for everything: I am very glad to be able to add a word to that painfully superficial farewell of last evening. I shall think of you with mingled feelings till I see you—at Beverley![3] Believe in my devotedly good wishes & regrets. Very gratefully yours

H. James jr

NOTES

1 The Paris address is handwritten, while the printed address (3 Bolton Street Piccadilly W) is crossed out. In September the Gardners, James and the Adamses seem to have enjoyed each other's company, according to Mrs Adams: "Friday [September 12th], Mr James, Henry, and I dined at a café, and then passed the evening at a café chantant in the Champs Elysées and were quite amused." On the Saturday: "Mr and Mrs Jack Gardner, Mr James, and we to dine in an open-air restaurant and then to the *cirque*, where Mademoiselle Jutan, an angelic blonde, filled our hearts with wonder and joy; then ices on the Boulevard in front of a café, and home at midnight" (*Letters of Mrs Henry Adams* p 178). Mrs Gardner also "presented in great form" Clover Adams to "the great Mr Worth" (pp 179–80). James saw the Adamses at dinner, and "three times a week" they went to the theatre. On the Adamses, see letter 6, note 3.

2 The Gardners visited the most important cathedrals of several French cities on this tour. Mrs Gardner would buy photographs of the various churches and monuments and glue them in her travel books or scrapbooks, adding dried leaves and flowers; see Carter p 51.

3 Beverly, in Massachusetts, Mrs Gardner's ocean-front house 'The Alhambra'. Jack Gardner's older brother Joseph P Gardner (1828–75) bought the house in 1863 and he willed it to his three sons, who were adopted by Isabella and Jack. William Amory Gardner (1863–1930) bought out his surviving brother in 1893 and became the sole owner. After Joseph's death, Isabella, Jack and the nephews seem to have spent the spring and early part

of the summer at Brookline, moving to Beverly around 1st July, staying into the fall. The house, originally on Mingo Beach, was moved inland and is now part of Endicott College. I owe this information to Richard Lingner, of the Isabella Stewart Gardner Museum.

The Adamses and the Hoopers were the Gardners' summer neighbours in Beverly Farms. (James mostly spelt 'Beverly' with an extra 'e'.)

VI

(Ms I S G M, Edel)

3, Bolton Street,
Piccadilly. W. *Jan. 29th* [1880]

My dear Mrs. Gardner
If you "like being remembered," it is a satisfaction you must be in constant enjoyment of—so indelible is the image which you imprint on the consciousness of your fellow-men. For me the pleasures of memory are also equally keen; but they are naturally rather active than passive. I remember those most agreeable days last summer in London & Paris—those talks & walks & drives & dinners—with a tenderness which the past, directly it recedes a little, always awakes in my sympathetic soul, but which in this case is altogether of exceptional softness. All those were delightful hours—not only pleasures, but treasures, of memory. I went a few nights since to another "smash"[1] at Lady Lindsay's[2]--just like the one you were at—; & as I moved about I seemed to feel your ghostly presence on my arm, & the sensation gave the affair an interest much finer than

the comparatively vulgar one which I trust I appeared to my neighbours to be taking. I have a happy faith that we shall Europeanize together again, in the future. But doubtless we shall, before that, Americanize; as I hold fast to my design of going home. I remained in Paris till Xmas—& never went to Italy, as I intended. But I shall try it this spring. London is more London than ever; there is a black broth, by way of atmosphere, & a kind of livid gloom, by way of sunshine, outside; I am incarcerated with a cold, & taking something, with a big spoon, out of a sticky bottle; & yet I am for the moment very cheerful & comfortable. I think of the *plaisirs* & the ginger-bread at St. Cloud!—The Adamses[3] are here, & have taken a charming house.—I am delighted you liked the little Hawthorne[4] (do you remember the day it was finished?)—& happy in the general appreciation you tell me of. You are dear kind people. Look out for my next big novel; it will immortalize me.[5] After that, some day, I will immortalize you.[6] Meanwhile, with very friendly regards to your husband, & love to those two jolly boys, I remain, my dear Mrs Gardner, very faithfully yours,

H. James jr

NOTES

1 James's 'smash' may suggest an analogy with the obsolete 'crash', to indicate a reception.

2 Caroline Blanche, Lady Lindsay (1844–1912), née Fitzroy, daughter of a Rothschild, poet and artist, the founder of the Grosvenor Gallery, with her husband Sir Coutts Lindsay (see letter 2, note 2).

3 Henry Adams (1838–1918), the famous writer and historian, well known for his autobiography, *The Education of Henry Adams*, published privately in 1907 (then in 1918), his essay *Mont Saint Michel and Chartres* (1904, 1913), his novels, *Democracy* (1880) and *Esther* (1913), the nine volumes of his *History of the US during the Administrations of Thomas Jefferson and James Madison* (1889–91). Henry Adams belonged to an illustrious Boston family, who had given two presidents to the United States. He married Marian Hooper (1843–85), known as 'Clover', in 1872. She had an important salon in Washington from 1877 (see letter 11). Clover was a bright and intelligent woman, with a great interest in photography. After the death of her father, Clover became seriously depressed, and committed suicide by drinking potassium cyanide—which she used for developing her photographs—on Sunday morning, 6th December 1885, in her home in Washington, DC. The Adamses were friends of Henry and of the James family. The Adamses arrived in Europe on 5th June 1879 (*Letters of Mrs Henry Adams* p 138), lived first at 33 Grosvenor Street, and in late June moved to 17 Half Moon Street Piccadilly W, with "Mr James in the next Street" (p 140). They left London at the beginning of August, travelled to France, Spain and Morocco;

they were back in Paris in mid-December 1879, and in London at the beginning of January 1880, returning to the USA and Washington in the autumn of 1881.

4 James's long essay on Nathaniel Hawthorne (1804–64), a writer who had a great influence on his early stories, was published on 12th December 1879 in England, and on 15th January 1880 in America (Edel-Laurence A12 a and b). The essay was not well received in the United States, as James complained to T S Perry on 22nd February 1880, see Edel *Letters II* p 274.

5 The novel is *The Portrait of a Lady*, published as a serial in 1880–81, and as a volume in 1881 (see letter 8).

6 James surely drew inspiration from Mrs Gardner (but certainly not only from her), her great wealth, her famous pearls, her love for the Palazzo Barbaro in Venice, which the Gardners rented several times after 1890, for the character of the heiress Milly Theale, in *The Wings of the Dove* (1902), and of the great collector, Adam Verver, in *The Golden Bowl* (1903).

VII

(Ms I S G M)

20 Quincy St.[1]
Cambridge, Wednesday. [9 November 1881]

Dear Mrs. Gardner.
If it really doesn't bore you, I shall be delighted to come & spend a night with you[2]—say tomorrow *Thursday.* If this shouldn't suit you I suppose you will have no difficulty in sending me a word by telegraph. If I hear nothing from you I will present myself in the afternoon, by some train that will bring me to Beverley at a discreet period before dinner. I don't suppose I need specify the train, (as I don't know about them,) for I shall have no difficulty in finding a conveyance at the station, & still less in walking to your house. You see I am taking you well at your word! It will perhaps teach you greater caution! With many good wishes. Very truly yours

H. James jr

NOTES

1 The Cambridge address, the town where Harvard is located, is written by hand. James sailed for the USA, after spending six years in Europe, on 20th October 1881. He lived in his parents' house, where his sister Alice also lived, at the Quincy Street address, and then moved to the Brunswick Hotel in Boston (Horne p 131).

2 In Mrs Gardner's summer house, at Beverly (see letter 5, note 3), about twenty miles north-east of Boston.

VIII

(Ms I S G M)

Cambridge. Mass.[1] *Nov. 17th.* [1881]

Dear Mrs. Gardner,
I should already have written you a line to thank you again for your gracious hospitality! But I started off for Newport[2] as soon as I got back here, & returned only last night: during which time I was not master of my moments even enough to scrawl you a hasty greeting. I was lunched, & dined, & supped & walked, & talked & driven, & generally appropriated—so that as soon as I took up the pen I had to drop it again. Newport is brilliant & beautiful (though the season is wholly defunct,) but it has not the sylvan sweetness of Beverley!

I take advantage this morning of sending you my last little book (which, this time, is rather a big one,)[3] to hope you are very well & are getting lonely in your little cabin-boudoir. In that case, as I go on Monday to Boston, one may, perhaps see you about town. Please receive the volume safely, but don't trouble to acknowledge it by the post. You can tell me that when you see me. Besides, then, perhaps, you will have read it. America seems to me more & more genial, & I trust I become so myself. Bore yourself a little—& give my friendly remembrance to your husband. Believe me also yours very gratefully & faithfully

H. James jr

NOTES

1 The address is written by hand.

2 Newport, Rhode Island, the famous summer resort frequented by New Yorkers and Bostonians, where the Jameses had lived in 1858–59. In the 1890s and at the beginning of the twentieth century, the 'vernacular' architecture of the simple homes of James's adolescence was being superseded by the huge stone and marble mansions of the new American tycoons, often copied from Italian Renaissance palaces or French chateaux. Going back to Newport in 1904, in *The American Scene* (1907) James described these 'cottages', as they were called, as "white elephants", luxurious dwellings looking "queer and conscious and lumpish—some of them, as with an air of brandished proboscis, really grotesque". These huge, new houses were seen as representing a "distressful, inevitable waste" (*American Scene* p 224).

3 *The Portrait of a Lady* (see letter 6).

IX

(Ms I S G M)

Parker House[1]
Thanksgiving Day. [1881]

Dear Mrs. Gardner
I am most annoyed & disgusted that the big little book should not yet have reached you. The order was sent to the publishers the day (or two,) before I wrote to you; & should immediately have been attended to. I will instantly look into it, & you shall receive the volume.—
I am delighted to hear that you are coming to town so soon, & shall lose no time in waiting on you, as you kindly propose. I shall be sure to turn up on Tuesday or Wednesday. If you are in town *before* the 1st Dec, I am afraid that day will again become the limit of my stay. But that is not till the end of the week. How very becoming this snowstorm must be to you!
Yours, with all the good wishes of the season, very faithfully

Henry James jr

NOTE

1 The address is written by hand. The Parker House, at the corner of Tremont and School Street, just off the Boston Common, was a famous hotel where the literary 'Saturday Club' of Ralph Waldo Emerson met, and where *The Atlantic Monthly* was founded. Charles Dickens stayed there during his American visit in 1867.

X

(Ms I S G M, Edel)

New York
115 East 25th Street[1] Dec. 7*th* [1881]

Dear Mrs. Gardner
I didn't come in, after all, that last day, as perhaps you noticed; I was so hard pushed to get away that evening that I hadn't time even to ring your bell & run away & then, too, I thought it probable Mrs. Palfrey[2] would be there, or if not Mrs. Palfrey, some other of *ces dames*, so that I shouldn't see you—to call it seeing you—after all. I therefore said to myself—"I will write her a little note; and that will make it up!" Here, accordingly, is the little note. You will say it has been a long time coming—& my only answer to that can be that time goes so fast in New York. I have stepped into a network of engagements[3] made for me by my genial host (Godkin,)[4] & have barely been able to lay my hand upon the fleeting hour & say "this is my own." New York seems to me very brilliant and beautiful, & the streets amuse me as much as if I had come from

Hartford, Conn.—or Harrisburg, Penn—instead of from London & Paris—& Boston! I have dined out every day for a week, & found the talk & the entrées equally good. Last night I was at a pleasant feast with three lovely ladies without their lords—Mrs. Butler Duncan, Mrs. Charles Post & Mrs. Baldy Smith—the males being Charles Strong[5] (the host,) Godkin, & my susceptible self. These ladies were charming, but what made most impression on me was that we talked of you. They wanted to know about you—they had heard you were so original! I gave a sketch—with a few exquisite touches—& then they sighed & said to each other: "ah, if we only knew how to be like that!" But they don't! I hope very much that your husband is doing well, & send him my hearty good-wishes. Have you found your ink-bottle as yet? If so, I should greatly value a few drops from it. Or if you haven't, even a lead-pencil might trace a few lines which though not indelible in themselves, would not easily be effaced from the memory of yours very faithfully

H. James jr

NOTES

1 The printed address is that of E L Godkin's house, where James was staying, while 'New York' was added by hand.

2 Anna Palfrey, a dear friend of the Gardners, whom she often visited, as is also evident from Mr Gardner's diary.

3 James had had a great success with *Portrait of a Lady* (see letter 6).

4 Edwin Lawrence Godkin (1831–1902), a friend of James's, was a journalist, Irish born, who acquired some fame with his reports during the Crimean war. He wrote for the *London Daily News*, about the South of the USA, also after emigrating to the USA in 1856. He then wrote for the *London Daily News* and the *New York Times*, and founded *The Nation* in New York City in 1865. He edited it until 1899, having sold it to the *New York Post* in 1881. The *Nation* became known for its campaign against political corruption and in favour of social reforms.

5 Mrs Butler Duncan was the wife of William Butler Duncan (1853–1933); Mrs Charles Post was Mary Minturn, the cousin of Minnie Temple (1845–70), James's beloved cousin who died very young, partly the 'germ' for the character of Milly Theale in *The Wings of the Dove*; Mrs Baldy Smith was Sarah Ward Lyon, of New York, the wife of William Farrar Smith (1824–1903), known as 'Baldy', a volunteer during the Civil War, then president of the International Telegraph Company, and after 1881 a civil engineer. He wrote an autobiography, *Autobiography of Major General William F Smith, 1861–64*, published posthumously. For Mrs Strong, see p 101 note 3.

XI

(Ms I S G M, Edel)

Metropolitan Club
Washington. D.C.
(723 15th St.)[1] *January 23d* [1882]

Dear Mrs. Gardner.
Why shouldn't I put into execution to-day that very definite intention of writing to you from Washington? I have been [here] nearly three weeks & I ought to have a good many impressions. I have indeed a certain number, but when I write to you these generalities somehow grow vague & pointless. Everything sifts itself down to *one* impression—which I leave to your delicate imagination. I shall not betray it if I can help it—but perhaps I shan't be able to help it.—Washington is on the whole as pleasant as you told me I should find it—or at least that you had found it. I try to find everything that you do, as that is a step toward being near you. I went last night to the Lorings[2] where you told me you had flung down your *sortie de bal*[3] in the dusky entry, where it looked like a bank of hyacinths,-& found

there the repulsive & fatuous Oscar Wilde,[4] whom, I am happy to say, no one was looking at.—Washington is really very good; too much of a village materially, but socially & conversationally higher & more varied, I think, than anything we have. I should care to live here[5]—it is too rustic & familiar; but I should certainly come here, for a part of every winter if I lived in the U. S. I have seen a good many people, dined out more or less, & tried to make myself agreeable. The Adamses[6] tell me I succeed—that I am better than I was in London. I don't know whether you would think that. I have not fallen in love nor contracted an eternal friendship, though the women, as a general thing, are pleasing. The most of a personage, among them, is Mrs Robeson,[7] but she is fifty years old & fundamentally coarse. Very charming, however, & with a *désinvolture* rather rare chez nous. There are also some charming girls—not rosebuds; e.g. Miss Bayard[8] and Miss Frelinghuysen,[9] who are very happy specimens of the *finished* American girl—the A.G. who has profited by the sort of social education that Washington gives. Plenty of men, of course; more than elsewhere, & a good many energetic types; but few "accomplished gentlemen." I met the President[10] the other day, (at dinner at Mr Blaine's)[11] & I thought him a good fellow—even attractive. He is a gentleman & evidently has that amiable quality, a desire to please; he also had a well-made coat & well-cut whiskers. But he told me none of the secrets of state & couldn't judge of him as a ruler of Men. He seemed so genial, however, that I was much disposed to ask him for a foreign mission. Where would you prefer to have me? I wish the States, over here, would send each other ambassadors—I should like so much to be at the head of a New York legation in Boston.—I see a good deal of our excellent Adamses, who have a very pretty little life here. Mrs A. has perennial afternoon tea—two or three times a day—& frequent dinners at a little round table. I remain here till the middle of February, & after that I go back to New York for a fortnight. Then I go to make a little tour in the South, & c; & *then*—& *then*—I should tell you if I were not afraid of betraying that emotion I spoke of in beginning. I hope you will be very amiable during the month of April, which I expect to spend in the neighborhood of Boston. I almost betray it there, & I must control myself. I hope you are having a genial winter--& should be delighted to hear a little about it. I venture to take for granted that your husband is completely recovered & that you have never failed to be well. I remain very faithfully yours

H. James jr

NOTES

1 The street address is added by hand to the printed heading for the Metropolitan Club. James went to Washington at the beginning of the year, meaning to stay for a few months, but he left for Boston after receiving a letter from his brother Robertson, who wrote that their mother was ill. James arrived in Cambridge on 31st January, two days after her death (Horne p 136). See letter 12.

2 The family of Judge Edward G Loring, dear friends of the Jameses. Katherine Loring was a close friend of Alice James; see letter 22.

3 A velvet evening cloak, doubled in silk, in fashion at the time.

4 Oscar Wilde toured America in 1882, attracting huge audiences and raising people's curiosity with his dandy's clothes and attitudes, which was reported spasmodically in the press. With "well-fitting velvet jacket" and "flowing white tie, lace cuffs, shirt studs, gold fob, and, most of all, his celebrated knee-breeches, completed by silk stockings and patent leather evening pumps" (Blanchard 1998 p XI), he impersonated the arrival of 'aestheticism' in America. His huge success was accompanied by great criticism, which appeared in the form of letters to the newspapers and caricatures; Julia Ward Howe (see note 6) received him at home in Boston and defended her right to do so in a letter to the *Globe* (15th February 1882), against a protest letter by Colonel Higginson. Howe's invitation caused a diatribe in conservative Boston and in the newspapers (McCauley *Gondola Days* p 49). On the great importance of Wilde's

aesthetic theories in the USA and his publicity skills, see Mary Warner Blanchard *Oscar Wilde's America*.

James describes Wilde here as "repulsive & fatuous", and, in a letter to Godkin, as "an unclean beast" (Horne p 135), but in fact he went to see Wilde after meeting him, to thank him for his public praise of his (James's) novels, even though their meeting was not at all successful (Ellmann p 179). James and Wilde shared many aesthetic theories, and they had both written praisingly on the same paintings by Burne-Jones (see letter 2). James's possible homosexuality and his absolute cult of privacy would make him very wary of any person publically acknowledging homoeroticism. On James and British aestheticism, see Freedman and Izzo.

5 James perhaps forgot to put in a negative.

6 See letter 6, note 3. James made most of his Washington acquaintances through the Adamses. Mrs Adams refused to receive Wilde: "I have asked Henry James *not* to bring his friend Oscar Wilde when he comes, I must keep out thieves and noodles or else take down my sign and go West" (18th January 1882 *Letters of Mrs Henry Adams* p 328). Mrs Gardner instead lunched in Boston with Wilde, who had been invited by Julia Ward Howe (1819–1910), a famous feminist and writer, and best-known as the author of *The Battle Hymn of the Republic*. Mrs Gardner kept an autographed photo of Oscar Wilde.

7 Mrs Mary I Ogston Robeson, the wife of New Jersey Senator George Maxwell Robeson (1829–97). She supported Wilde's visit to Washington.

8 James described the Bayard girls to his mother: 'such as one ought to marry, if one were marrying' (Edel *Letters II* p 371).

9 One of the daughters of Secretary of State Frederick Theodore Frelinghuysen (1817–85).
10 Chester A Arthur (1829–86), twenty-first President of the United States (1881–85). James wrote to his mother that the president thought Henry was the son of his uncle William (James's father's brother, and a clergyman), adding "this illusion was indeed apparently so dear to him, that I felt that if I had any smartness in me, I ought, striking while the iron was hot, to apply for a foreign mission, which I should doubtless promptly get" (Edel *Letters II* p 371). In January 1905, James dined again with an American president, Theodore Roosevelt, at the White House; see *The Correspondence of William James, William and Henry* III p 280.
11 James G Blaine, Republican, offered "a big and gorgeous banquet" for the president, as James wrote to his mother (Edel *Letters II* p 370).

XII

(Ms I S G M, Edel)

Cambridge,[1] *Friday.* [Feb. 3, 1882]

Dear Mrs. Gardner.
I thank you kindly for your tender little note, & am much touched by it. I have *felt* my dear mother's death[2] very deeply—I was passionately attached to her. She was sweet, gentle, wise, patient, precious—a pure & exquisite soul.

But now she is a memory as beneficent as her presence; & I thank heaven that one can lose a mother but *once* in one's life. The loss of that love, however, is a suffering absolutely apart—for it is the most absolutely unselfish affection any of us can know. Other forms of devotion seem to me comparatively interested. That of the being who went through nameless pain to bring one into the world & who has felt one's life in every fibre of her own being, is the purest essence of tenderness.—I shall come to see you one of these days, not long hence; & shall see you often, a little later, as I shall settle myself for a while in Boston. I wish to be near my father. Ever faithfully yours

H. James jr

NOTES

1 The address is written by hand.

2 Mary Robertson James (1810–1882), née Walsh, Henry James's mother, died on 29th January, of a bronchial asthma attack. James wrote about his mother's death in very similar words in his diary on 9th February 1882 (*Notebooks* pp 228–29). James received a note from his brother Robertson on 27th January, and arrived in Cambridge on the 31st, the day before the funeral (Horne p 136).

XIII

(Ms I S G M)

102 Mt. Vernon St[1] *March 29th* [1882]

Dear Mrs. Gardner.
So very, very kind …! I shall see you, in a day or two, the very first moment you are able—& tell you about the delicious little plan & the select very few. I most tenderly deplore your illness & rejoice in your convalescence. Most faithfully yours

H. James jr

NOTE

1 The address is written by hand, as it is in the following letters: 14, 15; in 16 and 17 it is placed at the bottom of the sheet, with the date. After Henry James's mother's death, the Cambridge Quincy Street house was sold and a smaller house in Mount Vernon Street, a very elegant address in the heart of Boston, was bought. James lived here from 9th February 1882.

XIV

(Ms I S G M)

102 Mt. Vernon St. *April 7th* [1882]

Dear Mrs. Gardner.

I am extremely sorry for your relapse—which is a relapse for all of us; but I cannot too strongly express the hope that you will conform rigidly to the orders of the ingenious & exasperating Bigelow.[1] On these terms we may perhaps see you again, with impunity, at an early date. It is a great novelty for us to find ourselves dangerous—though it mortifies us a little to reflect that we assume this character only as the hand of fate makes *you* defenseless! My little volumes will be innocuous at any rate: I hadn't them myself, & had to borrow them from Cambridge. Of the three *new* things (so to speak) they contain, the *Man of Fifty*[2] is the best. He wishes you a speedy & uninterrupted recovery & will soon come & see that it is going on. Very faithfully

H. James jr

NOTES

1 Henry Jacob Bigelow (1818–90), Mrs Gardner's doctor, and the father of William Sturgis Bigelow (1850–1926), who also studied medicine first at Harvard and then with Louis Pasteur in France, but never practised, going instead to Japan in 1882 with Ernest Fenollosa, becoming an expert on and a collector of Japanese and Oriental art, a Buddhist, and eventually donating over 40,000 Japanese art works to the Boston Museum of Fine Arts. Arriving in Japan in June 1883, the Gardners called on Sturgis Bigelow and then had dinner at his home with Mr and Mrs Fenollosa (26th June, John L Gardner *Travel Diaries 1883–84*).

2 James seems to be referring to the two volumes of 1879, *The Madonna of the Future and Other Tales*, since he writes 'three *new* things', which might be *Longstaff's Marriage*, *The Diary of a Man of Fifty* and *Benvolio*, which had only been published in a magazine, while the other three tales had been published in volume form (Edel-Laurence A10). In March 1883 *The Diary of a Man of Fifty* was reprinted in a new edition of *Daisy Miller*, no 303 of the Franklin Square Library, together with *An International Episode* and *A Bundle of Letters* (A8c). This last tale had been published with *The Diary* in 1880 (A14).

XV

(Ms I S G M)

102 Mt. Vernon St. *Wednesday*[1] April 12th [1882]

Dear Mrs. Gardner.
To come to you to be punished is almost a reward. I am delighted you are better. I shall give myself the pleasure of coming *tomorrow*, as I am obliged to go to Cambridge to-day. Be well, be happy, &, above all, be good! Very faithfully yours

H. James jr

NOTE

1 'Wednesday' is written sideways, at the top.

XVI

(Ms I S G M)

102 Mt. Vernon St *April 14th* [1882]

Dear Mrs Gardner.
I am shut up with a bad throat (it got much worse last night, & I have been in bed all day;) so that I am sadly afraid it wouldn't do for me to undertake our little performance[1] on Monday. It distresses me much to put it off—but won't you say *Thursday* instead?

Now that I am really taking care of myself I shall get better; but I shan't have any voice to speak of (or with) for three or four days. But I shall come & see you on one of the first of them & find you, I hope, in perfect health. Ever faithfully yours

H. James jr

NOTE

1 James alludes to his proposed reading of his play, drawn from his novel, *Daisy Miller: A Comedy*, which was privately printed by Macmillan in London, in July 1882, and paid for by the author, to secure its copyright; it was then published in *The Atlantic Monthly* in April–June 1883, and in volume form as *Daisy Miller: A Comedy in Three Acts*, by Osgood, in Boston, in September 1883. See Edel-Laurence A18 a and b.

XVII

(Ms I S G M)

102 Mt. Vernon St.
Sunday Noon.[1] [April 16th, 1882]

Dear Mrs. Gardner
You will be afflicted to hear that I am a good deal better, & have been out this morning. However, when I next see you I shall probably gratify you with the traces & ravages of misery. You remind me of a Roman Lady of the Decadence, at the Circus: I myself being the Christian Martyr! If your mysterious unknown[2] comes on Thursday I will with pleasure come on Wednesday (say) or Saturday: (I mean of course) if either of these days suits you; as to which I await further information.—I am not at all Roman—I am Greek! Therefore I delight in your, (I trust,) continued amendment. Ever faithfully yours

H. James jr

NOTES

1 Both address and time are added by hand at the end of the letter.

2 In this period novelist Marion Crawford was seeing Mrs Gardner, and causing gossiping hypotheses of a liaison. One wonders if the mysterious stranger was Crawford. See also letter 18. I am grateful to Richard Lingner for suggesting this possibility.

XVIII

(Ms I S G M)

Monday a.m[1] [April 17th, 1882]

Dear Mrs. Gardner.
Many thanks to the mysterious unknown. I will turn up on Thursday at seven—with my sermon in my pocket. I am getting odiously better. If you could be odious, I should hope the same of you. Bien à vous, Madame,

H. James jr

NOTE

1 This is added by hand at the end of the letter.

XIX

(Ms I S G M)

[April 1882]

Dear Mrs. Gardner.
I have just found your note, & am deeply gratified by your amiable impatience. I have, however, to my great regret made an engagement for Wednesday! Kindly contain yourself, & I will be, on *Thursday*, everything you can desire. I hope *you* haven't meanwhile made an engagement for Thursday! If I hear nothing more I will come on that day at seven. Many regrets for our incompatibilities—I am a Greek as I admire you—& a Xtian martyr as you persecute me. Ever

H. James jr

XX

(Ms I S G M)

102 Mt. Vernon St.[1] *April 24th* [1882]

Dear Mrs. Gardner.
I hope you may find health & happiness in New York. I am very sorry to say that on *Thursday* I am tied fast; but on *Friday*, at 7, if that suits you, I shall be delighted to come with my little entertainment. I await your orders—not your reproaches! Very faithfully yours

H. James jr

NOTE

1 Written by hand.

XXI

(Ms I S G M, Lubbock)

3 Bolton St.
Piccadilly. W.[1]
Reform Club
Pall Mall. S.W

June 5th [1882]

My dear Mrs. Gardner.
A little greeting across the sea!—I meant to send it as soon as I touched the shore; but the huge grey mass of London has interposed. I experience the need of proving to you that I missed seeing you before I left America—though I tried one day—the one before I quitted Boston—but you were still in New York, contributing the harmony of your presence & the melodies of your toilet, to the din of Wagnerian fiddles[2] & the crash of Teutonic cymbals. You must have passed me in the train that last Saturday; but you have never done anything but pass me—& *dépasser*—me: so it doesn't so much matter.—That final interview—that supreme farewell—will however always be one of the most fascinating incidents of life—the incidents that

didn't occur, & leave us to muse on what they might have done for us.—I think with extraordinary tenderness of those two pretty little evenings when I read you my play. They make a charming picture—a perfect picture—in my mind, & the memory of them appeals to all that is most *raffiné* in my constitution. Drop a tear—a diminutive tear (as *your* tears must be—small but beautifully-shaped pearls,) upon the fact that my drama is not after all to be brought out in New York (at least for the present.) I had a fundamental disagreement with the Manager[3] & got it back from him just before sailing. It is possible it may see the light here—I am to read it to the people of the St James's Theatre next week. *Please don't speak of this*. London seems big & black & horrible & delightful—Boston seems only the last-named. You indeed could make it horrible for me if you chose, & you could also make it big; but I doubt if you could make it black. It would be a fair & glittering horror—suggestive of icicles & white fur. I wonder if you are capable of writing me three words? Let one of them tell me you are well. The second—what you please! The third that you sometimes bestow a friendly thought upon yours very faithfully

H. James jr

NOTES

1 The Bolton Street address is written by hand.

2 Mrs Gardner loved Wagner's music and went more than once to Bayreuth (see letter 55).

3 The manager of the Madison Square Theatre in New York, owned by the Mallory Brothers, was Daniel Frohman. James's play was refused because it had "too much talk and not enough action"; see Kossman p 21. James commented on the "ridiculous negotiations" and the proprietors who "behaved like asses and sharpers combined" (*Notebooks* p 232). James had hoped the London Haymarket would stage it, but it all came to nothing. See Edel *Complete Plays* p 119.

XXII

(Ms I S G M, Edel)

3 Bolton St
Piccadilly.[1] *September 3ᵈ* [1882]

Dear Mrs. Gardner.

I have an unanswered letter from you of almost two months (or rather of exactly that period) old! I have become the more fond of it as the weeks have gone by, & have been unwilling to *part* with it, as I may express myself, by answering it. It is only the thought that I may possibly get another in place of it that gives me this courage. I write you from the depths of this stale & empty London, & you will read my poor words on that wondrous piazza of yours, the haunt of breezes & perfumes & pretty women. Read them to the breezes, read them to the flowers,[2] but *don't* read them to the pretty women! I don't know why I should give you this caution, however, as you are not in the habit of boring your visitors. There is nothing to tell you about London at this spacious & vacuous moment, except that it is very delightful. I have it absolutely to myself, & London to one's self is really a luxury. I have been paying certain country visits[3]—but as few as possible, & even them I have now abandoned & I am spending this still, cool Sunday in the metropolis. The purpose of this proceeding is the ingenious effort to "make up for lost time" (I lost a great deal during June & July.) I really don't think lost time ever *is* made up—one can save a few hours out of the future but one never can out of the past! Fix your thoughts on your future then—& *forget* your past—if you can. It is very quiet—though a man has just come in, most unexpectedly, to propose that we shall dine together. So we shall repair to a hot & somewhat disreputable establishment at about the hour you will have come out to listen to your creepers and tendrils rustle in the breeze of the Atlantic. You have had a hot summer but I pray you have had a merry one! My sister[4] writes me you kindly came to see her & were all freshness & grace. Your journey to Japan & India[5] is a *coup de génie*: won't you take me with you as your special-correspondent—& companion? (I mean special-companion.) Poor little *Daisy Miller*,[6] in her comic form, has been blighted by cold theatrical breath, & will probably never be acted. She will in that case only be published. But she had *two evenings'* success, & that amply satisfies your very faithful friend

Henry James jr

I hope your health has been perfectly serene. I go to Paris for the autumn, on the *12th*.

NOTES

1 The address is handwritten.

2 James is referring to Mrs Gardner's ocean house at Beverly. See letter 5, note 3.

3 Among James's country visits he went to Mentmore, Wimbledon and Shere (3rd August 1882 *Notebooks* p 230).

4 Alice James (1848–92), sister of the four James brothers, a 'voluntary' invalid, who followed the events of the world with great interest and intelligence. She went to Europe several times, and wrote a diary from 1889 to 1892, the year she died of breast cancer, diagnosed in 1891. The diary was 'published' in 1894 in four copies by Alice's friend Katherine Loring (for each surviving brother and for herself), then partly published in 1934, and published in complete form in 1964 by Leon Edel. Henry James was initially made "intensely nervous and almost sick with terror" by the diary, because of "the printedness-*en-toutes-lettres* of so many names, personalities, hearsays", but he appreciated the power and quality of the writing, as is clear from a letter to his brother William, written from Rome on 28th May 1894; see Edel *Letters IV* pp 479–80.

5 The Gardners left Boston on 21st May 1883, bound for California, from where they sailed to the East, in a trip inspired by the lectures of Professor Edward Morse, a great scholar of oriental cultures (Goldfarb p 10). During this trip, which lasted more than a year, the Gardners went to Japan, China, Cambodia, India and finally—through the Suez Canal—to Venice, where they arrived on 12th May 1884.

6 *Daisy Miller*, the play (see letter 16 and 21, note 3).

XXIII

(Ms I S G M, Edel)

Paris, Grand Hotel.[1] Nov. 12th [1882]

Dear Mrs. Gardner
Your gracious note of the end of last month, which came to me an hour ago (since when I have been reading & re-reading it,) is almost as "crisp" as one of those "silver days" of winter (happy phrase—may I have it for my next article?) I wish it had been longer & regret extremely that, as you imply, the cultivation of virtue should have the effect of abbreviating your letters. If this is really the case I beg you without delay to become vicious & diffuse! Apropos of such matters you see that I am in the city of vice, where I am leading the same innocent & unagitated life that I drag about with me everywhere. I have been spending the last two months in France, but six weeks of them have been passed—very agreeably—in wandering about the provinces—Touraine, Anjou, Poitou, Gascony, Provence, Burgundy.[2] I spent a fortnight on the banks of the Loire, examining the old châteaux

of that region—Chenonceaux, Chambord, Amboise, Blois &c—& having taken a fancy to such manner of life, pushed my way further & saw a hundred more castles & ruins, as well as cathedrals, old walled towns, Roman remains & curiosities of every sort. I have seen more of France than I had ever seen before, & on the whole liked it better. This has shortened my stay in Paris, for I return to my dear & dingy London on the 20*th* of the month. The autumn has been loathsomely wet, but since I have been here the weather has been rather shining & Paris has touched a certain place in my affections which only Paris touches. I don't imply by this that it is by any means the deepest place—that tender spot is like those compartments in a French railway carriage that are reserved for *dames seules!* But Paris has a little corner of my complicated organism & it has filled it fairly well on the present occasion. It filled it better, however, that time when you were here. I find the same rather threadbare little circle of our sweet compatriots, who dine with each other in every possible combination of the Alphabet—though none of their combinations spell the word satisfaction. That however is the most difficult word in the language—even *I* am not sure I get it right. I dined last night with Mrs. Strong[3]—I dine tonight with Mrs. Van Hoffman;[4] that is about the tenor of one's existence, though there are a few other things between. Did you ever meet Clarence King?[5] He is just below stairs (at this hotel)

& I have been down to bid him good morning. He is a delightful creature, & is selling silver mines & buying water-colours & old stuff by the million. I believe I am to breakfast with him & the good John Hay[6] (who is also very clever.) You see I am very national; do insist on that to people when you hear them abuse me—even when it's you yourself who have begun. You don't abuse me however when you say such nice things as you have done about my article in the *Century*.[7] I am delighted it should have transported you a little, & that perhaps—for a moment—your Beverly ocean looked like the flushing lagoon. The unhappy paper, however, like everything in American magazines when I don't see the proof, is full of odious misprints. Do kindly correct a few of them on the margin of your copy. On p.19, at the top (right) "hardly" after *Europa*, should be *surely*. *Thrives* on the same page, below (left) should be *thrones*. "Loveliest", same page, first line on the left, should be "*loneliest* booth, & c." On p. 12 on the left, "wavy-twinkling", which is idiotic, should be "many-twinkling", which is a shade less so. And just beside it, on the other column, the "bright sea light seems to flash", should be "seems to fl*u*sh"—which is a very different thing. *Not*, on p. 10, left ("light is not in the great square") should be of course *hot! Colours*, p. 13 (left) should be *colour*, which makes just the difference; & *streaked* ("the wrong way") on the column beside that, should be *stroked*. Furthermore, on the last page (left), the "beach at the Lido is lovely & beautiful" should be of course "lo*n*ely & beautiful." Excuse this horrid printer's letter, but it lacerates me to see my careful prose so disfigured. I have only mentioned some of the deformities. I agree with you that the portrait[8] is one of these—& if you can accept the disagreeable photograph from which it is taken, I will send you the latter when I get back to London. Howells's charming article[9] makes me *flush* not *flash*, all over. It was about this time that I paid you that little visit last year—in the sweet sunny American autumn with just a little growl of approaching winter in it. I remember the sea, the woods, the colour of the rocks & the sound of the waves. Also the colour of your sofas & ottomans & the sound of your conversation. Apropos of sound, what a hush must have fallen upon Beverly with that mutual silence of the Gordon Dexters![10] But it's better to be silent que de se dire des bêtises. The Point of View appears in the *January* Century.[11] I *believe* I have an article on *Du Maurier* in the December[12]—sure to be full of misprints. Please allow for them—you know mon écriture. It is a shame to bother you with any more of this. I only hope it will be legible to you that I am ever very faithfully yours

Henry James jr

NOTES

1 Written by hand. As James wrote in letter 22, he left for Paris on 12th September, and returned to Paris at the beginning of November after the tour mentioned in this letter.

2 The volume was *A Little Tour in France*, published on 5th September 1884, and first published as *En Province* in the *Atlantic Monthly*, July–November 1883, February–April 1884. Much of James's French travelling was a homage to different writers, starting with Balzac in Tour and Touraine.

3 Mrs Charles Strong was Eleanor Fearing, who lived mostly in Europe with her daughter, having become estranged from her lawyer husband. James met her in Rome in November 1869 (*Notebooks* Edel note 10 p 216)

4 Mrs Van Hoffman, whom James had known for several years and presented to Charles Peirce in Paris in 1876, was a French woman, living in New York, in Paris and in Rome at Villa Mattei (or Celimontano, on the Celio hill); see letter of 14th March 1876, *The Correspondence of William James, William and Henry* I pp 255–56, and letter of 19th May 1873 from Perugia ibid p 205.

5 Clarence King (1841–1901), geologist, a friend of John Hay and Henry Adams, the author of *Mountaineering in the Sierra Nevada* (1872) and Director of the US Geological Survey. He had a secret common-law wife, a black woman, Ada Copeland. He died of tuberculosis in Arizona; before going there he went to Washington for the last time: "The sunshine of life had not been so dazzling of late but that a share of it flickered out for Adams and Hay when King disappeared from their lives … " (*The Education of Henry Adams* Adams *Novels* p 1081).

6 John Milton Hay (1838–1905), a literary and political man; Abraham Lincoln's private assistant, a journalist, poet and novelist; ambassador to the United Kingdom (1897–98), Secretary of State (1898–1905) under Presidents William McKinley and Theodore Roosevelt; he supported the 'Open Door Policy' towards China (1899). With John N Nicolay he wrote *Abraham Lincoln, A History* (1890), in ten volumes. He was a friend of Clarence King and of Henry Adams. The Architect Richardson was commissioned to build houses in Washington for John Hay and Henry Adams. Sargent painted his portrait in 1903. See Ormond-Kilmurray 2003 pp 98–99.
7 The essay *Venice*, published in *The Century Magazine* xxv November 1882 pp 3–23. James lamented its "hideous misprints" in a letter of 27th November 1882 to Howells, when sending him the essay; see Anesko p 236.
8 This issue of the *Century Magazine* also printed a portrait of Henry James (p 24). William James found it a "very good portrait"; see *The Correspondence of William James, William and Henry* I p 337.
9 William Dean Howells wrote a long article, *Henry James*, on James's work, also published in this issue.
10 Mr Franklin Gordon Dexter (1824–1903), a Bostonian, was involved in railroad construction in the West and became a member of the board of directors of the Union Pacific and Central Pacific Railroads. In 1903 his will provided that no woman descendant could share his wealth, as *The New York Times* reported in January. His wife was Susan Green Amory (1840–1924), descendant of Martha Amory Babcock, the

biographer of John Singleton Copley. There was also shipping in the family (one F Gordon Dexter had married Harriet Appleton, daughter of the owner of the shipping firm, in 1851) which may explain why he was in Japan in 1861, when he was entrusted by Dr Hall with "several Wardian cases filled with Japanese plants" (Spongberg) to take back to Boston and deliver to the care of Dr Francis Parkman, historian and horticulturist. I am grateful to Tom Carter, of the Salem Philips Library, for checking some genealogical data. The Dexters had a house and an estate at Beverly Farms. Their silence remains unexplained.
11 *The Point of View* gave different views of America and Europe through the letters written by different characters. It was published in February 1883, in the collection *The Siege of London*, which also included *The Pension Beaurepas* (Horne p 144). Clover Adams wrote that the only letter that "hit" her was that of the Hon Marcellus Cockerel, strongly critical of England, and pleaded "guilty" to one of the expressions used in it. (*Letters of Mrs Henry Adams* p 403).
12 The article *Du Maurier and London Society* was published in the *Century Magazine* xxvi May 1883 pp 48–65 (Edel *Letters III* p 410).

XXIV

(Ms I S G M)

131 Mt. Vernon St. *Thursday a.m.*[1] [4 January–5 April 1883]

Dear Mrs. Gardner.
That you should have thought I would come yesterday is perhaps remarkable; but that I should have thought you would think I would come—which I did think—is more remarkable still! It is not remarkable, however, that I should eagerly embrace your kind proposal to appear on Friday, tomorrow, at five. Very faithfully yours

Henry James jr

I deplore your sprained ankle. Vous n'avez pas de chance—except perhaps in surviving at all!

NOTE

1 Written by hand at the end of the letter. The letter has black edges for the death of James's father, in the early hours of 18th December 1882. The novelist arrived in the United States on the 21st; he would have been too late to see his father alive or take part in the funeral, even if he had left immediately on hearing about his father's illness. William was in Paris, working with Charcot, and from there he moved into Henry's apartment in London. Therefore William too was not present at Henry James Sr's funeral.

XXV

(Ms I S G M)

131 Mt. Vernon St.[1] *Friday p.m.* [5 January–6 April 1883]

Dear Mrs. Gardner.
I was on the point of going to see you to-day—a couple of hours ago—when I was stopped by the arrival of Randolph Robinson,[2] of New York, who planted himself on the sofa & staid for an hour—when it was too late. In the course of this hour however, he he expressed very ardently! the desire to make your acquaintance, & I accordingly told him that I would bring him to see you if I should be able to ascertain that you would be at home tomorrow Saturday, about 5.15. The only way to do so is to write you this hasty note & ask you if you will be so good as to let me know. He is here but for a couple of days. It won't be *my* visit, after all—but that will keep. I am to meet you at dinner on Wednesday. Very faithfully yours

H. James jr

NOTES

1 Written by hand.

2 Perhaps E Randolph Robinson, a Virginian living in New York, a lawyer, Godkin's ally "in fighting civic corruption in New York City" (Horne p 244 note 1).

XXVI

(Ms I S G M)

131 Mt. Vernon St.[1] *Thursday* p.m. [11 January 1883]

Dear Mrs. Gardner.
I shall be very happy indeed to go with you on Saturday to the play, & as Matinées begin, I believe, at two o'clock, I will come to your house at 1.30.[2] I hope you have seen the last things. That is I hope you have seen the Othello—but *not* the *Gladiator*,[3] which is a mistake. Your letter from Washington has just been returned to me from London—which I think very kind of *it*. Very faithfully yours

Henry James jr

NOTES

1 Address and day written by hand at the end of the letter.

2 The MS has 2:30 crossed out.

3 In January 1883 the *Boston Daily Globe* advertised the performances of Tommaso Salvini (1829–1915, Italian actor) at the Globe Theatre in *Othello* and in *The Gladiator* as Niger, and announced Salvini as King Lear. On 11th January, the *Boston Daily Globe* reported on the success of *The Gladiator* on the previous evening, to a full audience in spite of the "heaviest storm of the winter": "Salvini's impersonation of the savage Niger in whose heart love and revenge held alternate sway, proved as broadly effective and as masterful as ever. Indeed, the scene in the arena, where the gladiator passionately appeals to the people against the cruel emperor's decree, was presented last night with peculiarly vivid and striking power." *The Gladiator* was the English translation of a five-act tragedy by French poet Alexandre Soumet (1788–1845). James wrote at length on Salvini, both on his Boston performances of 1883, inclusive of *Othello* and *The Gladiator*, and of his London performances of 1884. See *Scenic Art* pp 168–91. Strangely, Salvini spoke in Italian, while the rest of the company used English; ibid p 170.

XXVII

(Ms I S G M, Mamoli Zorzi)

3 Bolton St. May 2d [1884]
Piccadilly.[1]

Dear Mrs. Gardner
I ought to have answered before this your terrible little letter from Agra[2]—but you mentioned the 1st May as the first moment, probably, at which you would find my own epistle (at Venice:) & I reflect that this is only May 2d & that people never arrive in Venice as soon as they expect to. As you must have been dallying with the Orientals on the way, you probably won't get there for another week or so.[3] I am myself, as you see, a striking example of the truth of that axiom—that one doesn't get to Venice as soon as one expected to the year before. I shall not get there for a long time, my dear lady—till a long time after you have left. I shall see you before that, here in London, & will then explain to you the source of my little delays.—You will talk perhaps about broken vows—or you would, at least, if you were not a woman of infinite tact. We

must break something, sometimes, & if I didn't smash a promise occasionally, I shld. fracture something more valuable still. I won't ask you to forgive me—for you will pretend you won't—even long after you have really done so—& the plea of extenuating circumstances sounds weak. I would much rather pose as a faithless friend—I so seldom have the opportunity. It is true that I haven't the excitement of believing that you miss me—on the lagoon—for I know too well that you don't miss anything or any one, in this preposterously pleasant career of yours. You have everything, you do everything, you enjoy everything, & if you don't happen to find the extra-post-horse at Venice to pull your triumphant car—to tow your gondola—you may be sure the poor patient beast will be waiting at the next *étape.* In other words I shall be waiting in London, & shall get into harness when you arrive. In the meanwhile have pity on the place where the collar has rubbed. I wear a collar always: *que dis-je?* I wear half a dozen. They are piled up round my poor old head, & when you see me you will scarce distinguish the tip of my nose. I am a ruminant quadruped, too, & I turn it over in my mind that, really, I, at least, am too good a friend of yours to lend a further hand—or hoof—in spoiling you. I have heard about the King of Cambodia—& the Nizam of Hyderabad (?)[4]—all about your adventures & entertainments & I feel kind of savage at the thought that you have had this lovely time while I have had a rude workaday life, jolting & scraping from one dull day to the other. I don't pity you, dear lady—though I appreciate you as much as ever. I send you herein a line from Mrs Bronson,[5] who, however, is so absurdly easy to know that you will throw it overboard. Take it out of me *here*, & believe me ever yours unfaithfully

Henry James

NOTES

1 Written by hand.

2 The Gardners arrived in Agra, India, on Friday 7th March 1884. See John L Gardner's *Travel Diaries.* On the trip to the Orient, see the catalogue *Journeys East, Isabella Stewart Gardner and Asia.*

3 As mentioned above (Introduction p 11), the Gardners arrived in Venice, from their tour around the world, by sea on 12th May 1884 (erroneously marked as 13th May by Jack Gardner in his diary), with some delay in their programme, as foreseen by James; they stayed at the Hotel d'Europe and the day after they had arrived they went to see the Curtises at Palazzo Barbaro.

4 James inserted a question mark, maybe wondering about the spelling. Mr Gardner had annotated in his diary after arriving at Hyderabad: 'We arrived abt 4 p.m. Had a tent. Camp very comfortable'. (*Travel Diary 1883–84* p 45).

5 Katharine de Kay Bronson (1834–1901), one of James's American friends, had moved to Europe and to Venice in 1875, living in a house on the Grand Canal, Palazzino Alvisi, across from the Salute Church, with her daughter Edith (1861–1950). She had married Arthur Bronson (1824–85), lived in Newport, travelled, but then opted for Venice, while her husband stayed in Paris, due to his mental illness. Mrs Bronson became a close friend of Mrs Gardner. James was her guest in 1887, in a side wing of the house, where Robert Browning was also a guest. Her house was an important meeting point for Americans in Venice, and also for young artists, such as Whistler. Mrs Bronson was an intelligent and very generous woman, who helped

the gondoliers' children, restored little Madonna capitals at the *traghetti*, and identified with the place where she had chosen to live to the point of writing plays in Venetian dialect. Some of her *commediette* were staged in Asolo, where Mrs Bronson bought a house, 'La Mura', having fallen in love with the place after reading Browning's poem *Pippa Passes* (1841), set in Asolo. In the last year of Browning's life she was very close to the poet, who dedicated his last book of poems, *Asolando*, published posthumously in 1890, to her. Her daughter Edith married the Florentine nobleman Cosimo Rucellai in 1895 and lived in Tuscany where Mrs Bronson died. James was a dear friend of Mrs Bronson's and wrote an essay on her house, *Casa Alvisi*, originally published as a prefatory note to Mrs Bronson's memoir of Browning in the *Cornhill Magazine* February 1902. Mrs Bronson's Palazzino Alvisi is also mentioned in James's essay *The Grand Canal* (1892).

XXVIII

(Ms I S G M)

3 Bolton St. W.[1] *June 21st* [1884]

Dear Mrs. Gardner.

Don't really say such cruel things to me! I am certainly not unkind—I am soft & humane—& I don't think I am frivolous.—I assure you I never dreamed of saying anything that would not seem to you essentially friendly, & if I took a jocose & evasive (!) tone, it was partly to conceal my irritation in not being able to get away from London, & partly to conjure away any little irritation *you* might feel by trying to amuse you a little. And to think that I only displeased you! Life is decidedly too hard, & it's no use trying.—I don't know who my "friend" may be who has served me so well—auprès de vous—by telling you that I am steeped in vanities here, & I hope that by this time he may have caught typhus fever, or have drowned in the lagoon, or tumbled from the campanile, or something of that kind. When I say he, I mean *she;* such malignity could only come from a woman. I am busier than I have ever been, & doing my best to stem the tide of London interruptions. It is true they are innumerable, & London is *hateful* to me in June & July. I loathe it more, every year, at this particular period, & there is therefore some truth in the rumour that I am trying to get away as soon as possible. Why do you come so late—to an exhausted & exasperated society? By the first week in July every one is hot, weary, cross, impatient, panting for the end, *épuisé*! I have a plan of going to the smallest & dullest hole in Switzerland on July 1st: but I shan't execute it—I can't—& if you come, I won't. I hope still to be here when you arrive, if you are not inordinately late, & if you will tell me that I am not frivolous & unkind but serious & tender, I shall be here also when you depart! I will drive with you in the gondola of London, the casual hansom, failing that of Venice. I hope your journey northward will be short & comfortable—& if I can do anything here before you arrive to facilitate your advent, I shall be delighted. Very faithfully yours

Henry James

NOTE

1 Written by hand.

XXIX

(Ms I S G M)

Wednesday [16 or 23 July 1884]

Dear Mrs. Gardner.[1]
There is a quick train for Windsor at 5.10, which gets there at 5.45. I think it would suit us, for if we dine at 8.15, we shall have 2 hours & ½ for our drive &c. This will suffice. There is a train back at 9.10 & one at 10.20. If the 2^d^ should be too late for you, we can, by dining at 8 o'clock, precisely, very comfortably take the 2^d^. Therefore I will call for you at 4.30 tomorrow. Very faithfully yours

Henry James

P.S. On the whole we should be hurried! Therefore as there is a (slower train) at 4—let us take that. I will call for you therefore at *3.30* *sharp*. Excuse my contradictions.

NOTE

1 James saw the Gardners in London, when they arrived from Venice after their trip around the world.

XXX

(Ms I S G M)

34, De Vere Gardens, W. *October* 21st [1886]

Dear Mrs. Gardner.
I hope this will just meet you on your arrival[1]—if your arrival takes place, as I gather from your note from Florence, to day. Let it convey to you the friendliest welcome & my intention of immediately coming to see you. I pant for the history of your adventures. Your Florentine note was absolutely void of *addresses*—otherwise I should have given you a sign of intelligence before this. It is now only my inference that you alight here at your former hotel[2]—an inference founded on a general faith—or shall I say simply hope? in your constancy—May it not fail yours ever faithfully

Henry James

NOTES

1 In June 1886 the Gardners had gone back to Europe: England, Bayreuth, Vienna, Venice (from 13th September), Florence (24th September–11th October) and London. On 13th July, they had lunch with James, as Mr Gardner annotated in his *Travel Diaries, 1886.*

2 The Albemarle Hotel (Kozol TS).

XXXI

(Ms I S G M)

34, De Vere Gardens, W. *October 26th* [1886]

Dear Mrs. Gardner
I am writing to Sargent to say to him that we will come & see Mme Gautreau[1] on *Thursday* at about *3.15.* I hope this will meet your views. I go out of town on Saturday, to stop till Tuesday—& you leave London, as I understand it, on that Wednesday. This leaves us therefore only Friday of this week—which is a small margin; & I am very busy both this afternoon & tomorrow—beside the time being short to prepare Sargent's mind & Mme Gautreau's body. In short I assume that Thursday will do. Don't answer this—as I expect to see you this afternoon. I only send a word in advance to give you a timely warning & let you know that the bolt is levelled at the susceptible young artist.
Ever very faithfully

Henry James

NOTE

1 James took Mrs Gardner to see the famous portrait of Madame Gautreau, which had created a scandal in Paris when it was exhibited as Madame X at the Salon. Such was the scandal, due to the pose and decolleté of the lady, immediately recognized as Virginie Avegno, married to the banker Gautreau, that Sargent in fact moved to London. There are several studies for this portrait, both in pencil and in watercolour. Mrs Gardner perhaps aspired to a similar portrait, and had one painted in 1888, with her wearing her black Worth gown (see letter 42, note 2), pearls and rubies around her waist and neck and rubies on her slippers. In 1919 Mrs Gardner also bought the oil painting, *Madame Gautreau Drinking a Toast* (c 1883): see Ormond-Kilmurray *The Early Portraits* pp 103–04, 113–18, and Kilmurray-Ormond 1998 pp 100–03.

XXXII

(Ms I S G M)

34, De Vere Gardens, W. *November* 5*th* [1886]

Dear Mrs. Gardner.

Mrs. Mason[1] shall have your message & a report of your conversation so accurate & vivid that she will *roar* with regret at what she has missed. And you shall have, once more, the blessing, on your way, of yours very faithfully (quietly roaring too, on this side, at what she loses)—

Henry James

NOTE

1 Alice Mason (1833–1913), from Boston, first married William Sturgis Hooper (1833–63), and then senator and anti-slavery leader Charles Sumner (1811–74) in 1866, from whom she separated in 1867, and obtained a divorce in 1873. James met her in Rome in 1873, when she was waiting for the divorce. For her biography and for the portrait painted by Sargent, see Ormond-Kilmurray *The Early Portraits* no 140 pp 142–43. She became a good friend of both Mrs Gardner and Henry James. See also letters 39 and 98 and notes.

XXXIII

(Ms I S G M)

34, De Vere Gardens[1] *July 22d 1887*

Dear Mrs. Gardner.
Will you hold out your beautiful hand in friendship to my very good friend Mr. Charles H. Robarts?[2] He is an old ally of mine, & you would have very little to do to make him one of yours. You have so many, I know, that you are not in want—but it would be a great advantage to him—& you are full of sympathy. Mr. Robarts will come to you by way of the West Indies—but I predict that the London quality that is in him & which you will particularly like, will not have evaporated when he has the pleasure of seeing you. He carries on the affairs of an island in the Southern Seas which you have probably visited under one of his predecessors—so that *he* returns you the visit. He has however seen me very lately here, & if you are kind to him (& there is no doubt you will be,) he will feel that he can afford to mention to you that I am always the most systematic, though alas the most distant, &, I fear, the most dim, of your satellites—

Henry James

NOTES

1 The address is written by hand, as it is in letters 34–41.

2 James met Charles Henry Robarts (b 1840) in London in February 1877, as he wrote to his brother William, and made friends with him, in spite of his first negative comments ("Tho' civil, he belongs to the type of Englishman one least endures—the big Englishman who looks like a superior footman, with a turn up nose & an indented chin", *The Correspondence of William James, William and Henry* I pp 280–81). Robarts was a barrister, with the address 9 Little Stanhope Street in Mayfair, London, in 1890, which Mr Gardner annotated in his June 1888 diary (*Travel Diaries*), and he presented James to the Reform Club in 1878. He himself was a member of the Reform Club from 1868 to around 1904–05, when he died. Robarts was introduced to John Hay by James in 1887 (see Monteiro pp 102–03). See letter 35 about the visit to Isabella Stewart Gardner.

XXXIV

(Ms I S G M)

34 De Vere Gardens.W.[1] *July 26th* [1887]

Dear Mrs. Gardner—
I have perpetrated such an outrage upon you that I hasten to make my confession & ask for absolution. I have in the same week given *2* individual letters of introduction to you. But don't be frightened & don't worry—& I will try to be equally calm. I think it highly probable that one of them, at least, will never be presented, as the bearer, a very good friend of mine, & original & pleasant person, has betaken himself to a small island on the West Indies (of which he is English governor or caretaker,) where the natives will devour him or he devour the natives—in either of which cases you needn't expect him. His name is Charles Robarts—he is very "well-connected"—has seen much of the world &c, as well as of public affairs in this country—& has not altogether passed the age at which one falls in love. That he has imagination—though he won't need that if you are even just a little

kind to him—is proved by the fact that he candidly begged me for letters in your neighbourhood—on the plea that he was going "to America." He is to reside, & has already resided (he has only been back here on a holiday) in the general vicinity of Hayti—However, he *is* capable of coming from there to see you, now that he really holds a passport in his hands. Think how doubly dazzlingly fair you will seem to him—& let him down easily. I don't really think he will bore you—or I shouldn't—I wouldn't—have given him even an introduction which I think him but little likely to use. On the other hand Paul Harvey[2] *may* use his. Paul Harvey is of *very* tender years—he has just left Rugby—he is going into the army—& is spending a few weeks in the U.S. in the care of an English parson whom I don't know, whom I have ignored in my note, & whom you are perfectly free to ignore. He has asked me—so wistfully—for a letter or two—that thinking him a very nice & gentlemanly boy, & having known him since he was an infant, I have bethought myself that you perhaps would say a few words to him if he crosses your path. He is a near relation of a very brilliant & interesting person, a French lady, of whom you may have heard—Mrs. Lee Childe[3] (I haven't written her name legibly—Lee Childe,) who was a very good friend of mine & died nearly 2 years ago in Paris. He is an orphan, quite exceptionally alone in the world (some day I will tell you his very curious history,)[4]

& since her death I have tried to be kind to him—the more that he is an attractive boy (of a very English type) & has distinguished himself at school. I don't quite know how he will get at you at Beverley—& perhaps he won't. I shan't shoot him at you too straight—That is my confession—it is rather abject. But I won't do it again!—I am almost this minute—that is, five days ago—back from my long stay (eight months,) in Italy. I was in Venice till July 1*st*—I don't say it to torment you.—England will now possess me—& I hope will appreciate the privilege, till next spring. Your name, in Venice, was still a good deal in the air—a very golden, rosy, delicious place for it to be. I can't ask you questions, for it would seem as if I were adding insult to injury by expecting you to write to me. I shall have tidings of you when I *recueillir* the disordered fragments, or at least the incoherent syllables, of Robarts & Harvey. I shall feel kindlier than ever to them then—poor things—Most inconsistently I feel so to you, dear Mrs. Gardner, & this is not a hollow phrase—it might be a much handsomer one—from yours ever faithfully

Henry James

NOTES

1 The address is written sideways.

2 Paul Harvey (1862–1948), the Marquis of Landsdowne's private secretary, British diplomat, and from 1909 financial advisor to the Egyptian Khedivé; he also compiled the *Oxford Companion to British and French Literature.* James admired his multifaceted personality (*Notebooks* p 304).

3 Harvey was the nephew of Blanche de Triqueti, married to Edward Lee Childe (1836–1911), whom James saw in Paris and in Varennes in 1876. In a letter to his mother James described the young Paul as "a lovely infant of about six years—a little orphan nephew of Mrs. Childe" " … has eyelashes six inches long and is a source of much delectation to me when the superior discipline of the house permits him to appear" (Edel *Letters* II pp 27, 62).

4 Paul Harvey was the son of a painter, Edward de Triqueti, and of a British governess.

XXXV

(Ms I S G M)

34 De Vere Gdns.[1] *Oct 19th* [1887]

Dear Mrs. Gardner.

It was very lovely of you to be so kind to poor stammering, exiled, unpopular Robarts—who wrote me that he had passed a day of enchantment in your society. He is banished, as I suppose he told you, to a lone nigger isle in the West Indies, where he lives on canned meats, & now, doubtless, on canned memories. It is most kind of you, further, to say that I *may* once in a while send you a Briton. I shall use this license most discreetly—as well as rarely—but once in a while it may be a blessing to have it, as I have no one now, in America save my poor brother William,[2] who is weary & overworked & whom moreover I have used in that way too much already. Paul Harvey never turned up, I know—he came & wept to me about it on his return. He was with a stupid friend who dragged him off to Canada, where he spent 2/3's of his time. Meanwhile he secretely pined for Beverly & came home a shadow.

I am sorry he lost you, as he is [a] very nice and attractive boy, with a very handsome face & a curious, mysterious, romantic history, which I will some day tell you. Meanwhile don't mention it! Mrs. Lodge[3] is here & I converse with her not infrequently—sometimes in the presence of Mrs. Mason, whom she is staying with—sometimes not. I am settled for the winter & trying to work. No Italy for many months: when are you coming back to the little perch over against St. James's St.? I wait at the foot of the ladder & am very impatiently & gratefully yours

Henry James

NOTES

1 The printed heading is that of the Athenaeum Club, Pall Mall, SW.

2 William James (1842–1910), Henry's older brother, the famous philosopher and professor at Harvard.

3 Anna Cabot Mills Davis Lodge (1850–1915), wife of senator Henry Cabot Lodge (1850–1924). With Mrs Cameron, she reigned in Washington for "sixteen years, during which Mrs Cameron and Mrs Lodge led a career, without precedent and without succession, as the dispensers of sunshine over Washington" (*The Education of Henry Adams* Adams *Novels* p 1024).

XXXVI

(Ms I S G M)

34 De Vere G^dns. *October 20th* [1887]

Dear Mrs Gardner.
It is very grotesque to have written to you only yesterday that I wd. avail myself of your kind permission to send you a Briton only *rarely*—& yet already to-day to be despatching you a specimen. Yes, I have just given a letter to you to the beautiful Harold Peto,[1] who sails in a day or two, & who is a good friend of mine. He is a young architect, held in considerable esteem professionally here & much liked personally, though—but you will discover the "though"—it won't mystify you. He goes to America only for a month, mainly to see buildings, & wishes particularly to see Boston. He is extremely amiable & pleasant, & won't bore or incommode you in the least. You will like him. Women usually consider him very good looking. He is the son of a certain Sir Morton Peto, of whom you may have heard, who made a great flash in the pan, as a kind of British railway king,[2] some years ago—& then went

out in (I think) some slight bad odour. But this boy is virtuous & pure. I am afraid he won't find you in Boston, but I have told him how to communicate. I don't send him to you to get rid of him—but because he will really entertain you. Ever faithfully

Henry James

NOTES

1 Harold Peto (1854–1933), well-known British architect. After Harrow, he studied architecture and worked in Sir Ernest George's office till 1895. Between 1902 and 1910 he designed several villas on the Côte d'Azur, among which was Villa Sylvia, Ralph and Lisa Curtis's home.

2 Sir Samuel Morton Peto (1808–89), the builder of many railways, including that of the Crimea (1854), was made a baronet for his industrial merits, but in 1866 he had a financial crisis which obliged him to give up his place in Parliament.

XXXVII

(Ms I S G M)

34 De Vere Gardens W. *October 20th* [1887]

Dear Mrs. Gardner—
I have already written—or you will have already received, a word from me about my friend Harold Peto,[1] who will give you this & require a very small opportunity to recommend himself. Being architectural himself, he seeks for architecture in others—& you are that, as you are everything. I want him to be much pleased with Boston, which I love so much, & this favourable view will come to him in perfection in your hands. Show him the gems—especially your own. I don't know whether he will find you at Beverly or at Brookline[2]—not, I surmise, in town. In case you are still by the sea the occasion will be good to show him the way to some of the new houses on your lovely shore—from which however I fear that by November 1st the occupants will mainly have departed. Even if you are not in Beacon St. mightn't he have a view of the inside of your so charming house there? And of other charms inside & out. He will deserve it all. Yours very faithfully

Henry James

NOTES

1 See letter 36, note 1.

2 'Green Hill', at Brookline, was Isabella Stewart Gardner's home outside Boston, while 152 Beacon Street was her town house, given to her by her father on her wedding. The Gardners lived there for nearly forty years, from 1862. The double house was rebuilt when Fenway Court was ready in 1902.

XXXVIII

(Ms I S G M)

34 De Vere Gardens, W. *December 5th* [1887]

Dear Mrs. Gardner—
Yes indeed, I remember well the day—the spring Sunday, we lunched together at poor Ellen Gurney's.[1]—Was there ever anything so tragical—so *melting?*—But I can't write of it or talk of it—I can only think of our long, charming acquaintance with her, & of the sweet, noble thoroughly fine woman that she was & try & pick her image up out of all this dark, dreadful violence & misery of the close—& put it away among the things that memory is tenderest of. But it remains the most poignant horror!—Let me thank you for your evident kindness to Harold Peto. He will be coming back quite soon now—& will tell me all about you & quicken that gratitude. Perhaps he will make me feel like an ass that I don't go over. Your hospitality must have made a great difference to him—& my consciousness of it—to the wandering Briton who wrenches a note out of me ere he starts—makes, dear Mrs. Gardner, to yours ever faithfully

Henry James

NOTE

1 Ellen Sturgis Hooper Gurney (1838–87), sister of Clover Adams, married Ephraim Whitman Gurney (1829–86), professor of modern languages and history at Harvard (*The Complete Letters* I p 174). Here James refers to her tragic death: she wandered onto the railroad tracks and was hit by a train, and died from the injuries on 20th November 1887. See *Letters of Henry Adams* III p 66 n 3. There has been much speculation regarding the suicides and the streak of depression running in the Hooper family; on her sister Clover's suicide, see letter 6, note 3. Their brother, Edward, leapt from a third floor window in 1901, and died two months later. James wrote with great affection of the Gurneys, who lived in Cambridge, in a passage of memories in his *American Journals*; see *Notebooks* p 242.

XXXIX

(Ms I S G M)

34 De Vere Gardens W. *March 18th 1888*

Dear Mrs. Gardner.
Welcome back to the world[1] that loves you best—I should have written you this six days ago, but that I have been buried up to my neck in proof-reading[2]—I just dash out an affectionate hand & wave it at you now. Please see all sorts of friendly "intentions" & expressions in the movement. What a wonderful Mrs. Jack-in-the-Box[3] you are—popping up, with all sorts of graceful effects & surprises, purely your own, in the most unexpected parts of the Universe. And always on the way to do something delightful. I envy you Spain—& envy Spain you. But why put so many Pyrenees & things between yourself & Piccadilly? My feet expect to tread that romantic avenue for many weeks to come, & indeed for many months—It is very perverse of you to talk of coming here in August—but after all it is not impossible that I may be in & out at that moment. My plans till then are unimaginative—

unless I go to Ireland for June & July.[4] That I call really fanciful. Do give me a good warning of your approach—so that I may fly—fly back, of course I mean. Harold Peto becomes quite energetic when he speaks of you. The placid mirror of his countenance seems literally to crack with enthusiasm. You must see that mirror in the delicate frame of his wonderful little house. Mrs. Mason is at Monte Carlo, morganatically, & *I*, with no other *soutien*, romantic or prosaic, than the hope of your advent, am ever affectionately yours

Henry James

NOTES

1 The Gardners were again in Europe. They went to the *feria* of Seville, where they saw Ralph Curtis (24th March John L Gardner *Travel Diaries*) and to Madrid, where they bought a painting by Zurbaran; they proceeded to Venice (arriving on 18th June) and Bayreuth (July, see letter 40), then to Brussels and to London, where they arrived on 29th July.

2 The proofs of *Partial Portraits*, published on 8th May 1888.

3 "Mrs Jack" was one of the ways in which Mrs Gardner was referred to, after her husband's nickname.

4 James did not go to Ireland; see letter 40.

XL

(Ms I S G M)

34 De Vere Gardens W.[1] *July 27th* [1888]

Dear Mrs. Gardner.

Oh yes, I shall be here: if not on that day certainly on the next—or next but one. But you must emit another cry—to the tune (Wagnerian, as you will be fresh from Baireuth)[2] of "Here I am". How kind of you to give me a glimpse of that scene with the feudal Countess[3] when she gave you the chance of shaking hands over the "love" of H.J. Hands forsooth! the close embrace, the comprehensive encircling, make a beautiful picture. I haven't been to Ireland[4]—she couldn't wait & came to London. They always do—I won't point to any more examples! It began to rain three months ago & my umbrella has not been *down* since then. The courage has been quite drowned out of me for leaving the shelter of streets & hansoms. Don't fail to let your signal be punctual & believe me ever faithfully yours

Henry James

NOTES

1 The address is at the end of the letter.

2 'Baireuth' is the spelling also used by Henry Adams.

3 The episode has not been identified.

4 Maybe a reference to Lady Kenmare (1840–1913),who lived at Killarney, County Kerry, in Ireland, and travelled to Venice to stay with the Curtises quite often.

XLI

(Ms I S G M)

34 De Vere Gdns W. *March-20th*: [1889]

Dear Mrs. Gardner.
I am at my old tricks again—forgive me. This time it is under particularly heinous circumstances, as I don't *know* personally Arthur Clough:[1] I only know many of his friends and his mother, his sister, & the great & charming fame of his father, which you will also know—the beautiful past of 20-30—years ago. I am told Arthur Clough (Clough)[2] is a particularly nice fellow, & the person who has directly asked me for an introduction for him, to the most charming woman in Boston, is a very old friend of mine & of many people in Boston—or rather in the U.S. at large, Sir John Clark, of Tillypronie, a most hospitable Scotch laird.[3] I have declined giving Clough a *letter*—but he has instructions to call on you, with the assurance that I shall meanwhile have prepared your mind. He will therefore turn up—be merciful to him. Mrs. Earle,[4] my nominee of last summer, passed through Boston

before you had returned to America. I fear *this* youth may find you flitted southwards. Please find in these hasty lines more sentiments than superficially appear; & some indication of how easily you happen to be present in the mind of yours most faithfully

Henry James

NOTES

1 Arthur Clough, the son of Arthur Hugh Clough (1819–61), a British poet who participated in the 1848 revolutionary movements in Italy.

2 In the MS James rewrote the name more clearly in parentheses.

3 Sir John Forbes Clarke (1821–1910), of Tillypronie, Aberdeenshire, Scotland, a diplomat until he resigned in 1855, and a good friend of the novelist. James described this "tenderly hospitable couple" to his sister Alice, on 15th September 1878, while he was a guest at Tillypronie, "among the brown and purple moors" (Edel *Letters II* p 184). In *English Vignettes* (1879) James wrote about the place, without naming it: " … a half-modernized feudal dwelling, lying in a wooded hollow—a large concavity filled with a delightful old park. The house had a long gray façade and half a dozen towers, and the usual supply of ivy and clustered chimneys relieved against a background of rook-haunted elms" (p 199). James was again a guest in 1881; see Horne p 84. After his wife's death, in 1909, Sir John published *The Cookery Book of Lady Clark of Tillypronie*, to great success, of Lady Charlotte's selection of recipes of special courses she had enjoyed at the dinners to which she had been invited.

4 Perhaps Mrs C W Earle, née Maria Teresa Villiers (1836–1925), author of gardening books. Mrs Gardner was a very keen gardener. See *Notebooks* p 58.

XLII

(MS I S G M, Mamoli Zorzi)

H. de la Ville, Milan[1] *May 15th* [1890]

Dear Mrs. Gardner.
Your truly attractive note, which overtakes me at this place this morning, exercises its attraction unimpaired over channels & alps. I left London but three days ago, with unconscious & (to myself injurious perversity,) at the very moment you were reaching it. But of course you are coming down here. By "down here" I mean to the sweetest land on earth—I care not with which you compare it. Don't waste time—& your figure—on Mr. Worth[2] & Paris, but come & feel with me—somehow & somewhere—the truth of the axiom just enunciated. Let your figure be reflected in the clear lagoon, say, sometime after June 1st.[3] It will meet mine in the same soft element & perhaps condescend to be occasionally seen in juxtaposition with it. Before June 1st I move about—going to as many little brown cities as I can: but for June I hope to float. Therefore come, if you won't sink me. At any rate I hope very much you'll be

in England the last half of the summer—for I return the 1st days of August, when the London season is over. Ever faithfully yours

Henry James

De Vere Gardens always follows me.

NOTES

1 Written by hand, on paper headed 34 De Vere Gardens, W; this explains the postscript.

2 The British couturier Frederick Charles Worth (1825–95), who in 1858 opened his atelier in Paris, at 7 Rue de La Paix, becoming very fashionable particularly after he provided dresses for Empress Eugenie, wife of Napoleon III. His sons Gaston and Jacques continued his work. Mrs Gardner bought her clothes at Worth's; she was portrayed in a Worth gown in her portrait by Sargent. In his novel *Democracy* (1880), Henry Adams has a wonderful and ironic description both of the creativity of Worth and of one of his ball dresses, ordered by the favourite of the King of Dahomey, *and* by Sybil, the sister of the protagonist, in Washington. After a sleepless night of worrying about the dress, Worth looks out of the window at dawn: "There before his blood-shot eyes lay the pure, still, new-born, radiant June morning. With a cry of inspiration the great man leaned out of the casement and rapidly caught the details of his new conception … An imperious order brought to his private room every silk, satin, and gauze within the range of pale pink, pale crocus, pale green, silver and azure. Then came chromatic scales of colour; combinations meant to vulgarize the rainbow; sinfonies and fugues, the twittering of birds and the great peace of dewy nature; maidenhood in her awakening innocence; 'The Dawn in June.' The Master rested content." He then replicates the dress as 'L'Aube, Mois de Juin', thinking it unlikely that the King of Dahomey should go to Washington and see the duplicate there (Adams *Novels Democracy* p 144).

3 James went to Venice in June, a guest of the Curtises at Palazzo Barbaro. The Gardners went to Madrid, London (July), Venice (1st August to early September).

XLIII

(Ms I S G M, Edel, Mamoli Zorzi)

Garmisch
Bavaria[1] *June 24th 1890*

Dear Mrs. Gardner.
There are many things I must ask you to excuse. One of them is this paper from the village grocer of an unsophisticated Bavarian valley. The others I will tell you when we next meet. Not that they matter much; for you *won't* excuse them—you never do. But I have your commands to write & tell you "all about"—something or other—I think it was Venice—& at any rate Venice will do. Venice always does. Therefore I won't give you further grounds for rigour by failing to obey your behest on this point. I have just been (3 days ago) to see the Passion Play at Oberammergau[2] & with my good friends & hosts the Curtises, with whom, 12 days ago, I left Venice to drive hither, delightfully, through the Venetian Alps, the Dolomites, Cadore, Cortina, the Ampezzo, &c., I am resting, after that exploit, in this sweet recess among the mountains—which has

been (it is but 2 hrs. away by carriage,) our point de depart for the pilgrimage. Tomorrow we drive back to Innsbrück[3] & separate—they to go to England[4] & I back to Italy, for two or three weeks more. The Passion Play is curious, tedious, touching, intensely respectable & intensely German. I wouldn't have come if I hadn't been brought (by Mrs. Curtis & Miss Wormeley,)[5] & I shall never go again even if I *am* brought by syren hands. But all these Tyrolean countries are beyond praise—& the several days' drive was magnificent. Venice was cool, empty, melancholy & delicious. They "sprang" upon me (the Curtises) the revelation that you are to have the Barbaro for August, torturing me thus with a vision of alternatives & preferences—the question of whether I would give up the happy actual (the secure fact of really *being* there in June) for the idea of a perhaps even happier possible or impossible, the romance of being there in August. I took what I had—I *was* there—a fortnight. Now I am going back, to stay but a day or two, & then do some other things—go again for 10 days to Florence & to 2 or 3 Tuscan excursions. Why are you so perverse?—Why do you come to London when I am away, & away from it just when I come back? Even your bright presence there does not make me repent having fled this year from the Savage Season. You wouldn't have made it tame—so what good should I have got? I hope you have found it as wild as you like things. The Palazzo Barbaro is divine, & divinely still: don't make it spin round. If I am in Italy still when you arrive je viendrai vous y voir. But I take it you have arranged your court. My clothes are there still (I only brought a necktie here.) But I shall get them out of your way—you would perhaps pitch them into the Adriatic. I shall write to you again & am ever, dear Mrs. Gardner, most faithfully yours

Henry James

NOTES

1 Written by hand on a white, slightly shiny paper that does not seem so rough as James's description.

2 The popularity of the Passion Play in this period increased enormously; Mrs Gardner also went to see it. Victorians were particularly keen on theatricals of various types, tableaux vivants, dressing up, masked balls and, of course, historical paintings. Even James had "the fatuity to assume a quattro-cento dress (of scarlet and black)" at a Florentine ball given in honour of the King and Queen of Italy in Florence in 1887 (Edel *Letters* III p 184). He also wrote to Mrs Gardner about *her* masquerade (letter 56) and participated in the masked ball of Lady Wolseley in Dublin (letter 64). See Mamoli Zorzi 1999 and 2002. The Curtises and James went by carriage to Innsbruck, then by train, and again by carriage, as James wrote in detail to his sister Alice.

3 James mistakenly wrote Innsbruck with the *umlaut.*

4 To see their son Osborne (1858–1918), at Summerhill, Fakenham, Norfolk.

5 Katherine Prescott Wormeley (1830–1908), Ariana Wormeley Curtis's sister and the translator of Bourget, Dumas and St Beuve: a lady "who has lately been so incongruously—as a New England old maid, unacquainted with French—and other badnesses—mistranslating Balzac", as James wrote on 27th February 1887, to Sarah Butler Wister (Edel *Letters III* p 170).

XLIV

(Ms I S G M)

Paradisino Vallombrosa
Pontassieve
Toscana[1] Friday, July 31st [1890]

Dear Mrs. Gardner.
I write these few lines on the assumption that you reach the Barbaro tomorrow & that you will receive them in the course of the day. I haven't written before—for so long—because, since it has been apparent to me that I should linger in Italy till the present date you have been on the roads & I haven't known how to get at you. I have reasoned lately that Baring's things wd. await you at Venice. However, better late than never, if it isn't too late—& this is a hasty scribble to say that I shall be delighted to join you, as it were, at the Barbaro, if you can have me for 4 or 5 days. I have been on these relative & shady heights for the last fortnight—but must descend & must alas take my way back to the workaday world. But I should be sorry wholly to miss you as I pass. I rather dread the descent into the torrid plain; & having

been in Italy since May 13th I am feeling that I have had enough & to spare of the Italian summer. All the same I leave this place for Florence on Monday next, 4th, at the latest & in this case will, if I have an indulgent word from you in the meantime, take, at the said Florence, on the said Monday evening, to escape the long, scorching day-journey, the 9.30 p.m. *night-express*, for Venice. Could you kindly send me a telegraphic word, *on receipt of this*, as to whether you can still more kindly put me up for the fleeting hour? *Paradisino, Vallombrosa* is an all-sufficient telegraphic address; though the clerk at the office at Venice probably won't know that there *is* a telegraph up here unless he is authoritatively informed that such is the case. Add *Pontassieve, Toscana*, if he wishes it. Don't trouble to say more than "Yes, Tuesday"—*Sì, Martedì.* The night-express from Florence gets me in at a sadly early, but a comfortably cool hour of the a.m.—5.20. But I hope this won't exasperate you. My old friends the 2 Titas will, I am sure, not be reluctant to come to the station for me even at the said 5.20, & as I shall not reach the house before 6, at the earliest, Angelo[2] will not refuse me a bath & some tea. Then you will see me later—at your full convenience. You will have had many adventures & will do the Moor of Venice for me—a very fair, female Moor. I hope your husband bears the life well, & I am, dear Mrs Gardner, yours most impatiently

Henry James

NOTES

1 Written by hand. Vallombrosa was the seat of a famous monastery and a summer place for many elegant Florentine families.

2 Angelo Sitran, the faithful Curtises' butler; see Curtis Viganò in *Gondola Days* p 204. The two Titas were the gondoliers.

XLV

(Ms I S G M)

Vallombrosa *Saturday night* [1890][1]

Dear Mrs. Gardner.

I telegraphed you this evening to thank heartily for repeating the telegram of my sister's maid, which has determined me to start for England immediately; in other words I leave this place tomorrow at 5.30 & travel straight & fast: I interpret the telegram, reading between its lines, as urgent—as I know that there would have been urgency before she telegraphed at all. I have in fact feared something of the sort & vaguely expected it, as Alice has been ill for a month[2] & I have, at bottom been uneasy at stretching out my absence so long. I have staid on here from the dread of descending into the extreme heat of the lower regions. Kindly excuse this hurried & inadequate scrawl & believe how thoroughly disappointed I am at losing my little visit in Venice after all. I am consoled only by thinking that it couldn't have been long—I have so come to the end of my rope, & find besides that July & August in Italy don't agree with me. I have not been well these 2 days & think with a certain horror of my long, fatiguing journey. May your tenure of the Barbaro[3] be happy—may your Venetian August let you off easily. I shd. like to write more, but I have everything to do. So I can thank you only for all the hospitality I *haven't* been able to gather. Surely you will be in London again—to sail?—I shall be away from it little in September & October.—I am afraid some of my letters will come—or will *have* come to the Barbaro, though I telegraphed an hour ago to stop them. I shld.—I would—write to Angelo[4] to send them on to me, back to London, but don't trust him exactly with an English address—therefore I wonder whether you would kindly ask Gardner to have the great Xtian charity to re-address anything that may come to me, to 34 De Vere Gardens London, W. and give it to Angelo to post?—This is all very miserable—but be happy you, both of you, at least & believe me both of you, yours most disappointedly & defeatedly

Henry James

NOTES

1 July. Vallombrosa is written by hand.

2 Alice wrote in her diary on 12th September: "Twas no go! I went under on Saturday August 2nd and administered an electric shock to Harry which brought him from the Paradisino at Vallombrosa to immure himself, without a murmur, in my squalid indigestion. He avenged himself upon Katherine, who received his telegram on August 6th, and by September 2nd had dug me out and transplanted (me) to these comfortable quarters … " (Edel *Diary of Alice James* p 135). After being ill almost all of her life, with no diagnosis and many different treatments, Alice was diagnosed with a breast tumour and died on 6th March 1892. On Alice James, see Strouse ch 17.

3 The Gardners rented the Palazzo Barbaro for the first time in 1890 (1st August–2nd September), and returned to it several times, almost every other year. Mr Gardner annotated "Rent of Palazzo Barbaro, Venice (amo't fixed by myself) Paid DS Curtis July 16/90—*£ 200*' (John L Gardner *Travel Diaries, 1890* p 16). On arriving in Venice from Verona, on Friday, 1st August, Mr Gardner wrote joyously: "Installed at Palazzo Barbaro. Hurrah!" (ibid p 6).

4 See letter 44.

XLVI

(Ms I S G M)

Reform Club, Pall Mall. S.W. *August 9th* [1890]

Dear Mrs. Gardner.

A thousand thanks for your, & Gardner's, kind promptitude in having my letters sent back; & I am also grateful to you for your note of sympathy. I was met at Basle by news which enabled me to rest there a number of hours, but when I got to Leamington,[1] from which I have just returned, I found it was very well I had not delayed longer, as my sister was in a miserably suffering condition, & her isolation there is too great to make that, in such circumstances, anything but a rather serious crisis. At the end of two days, however, she got somewhat better & I have come back to town. I am happy to say that we are expecting, or at least hoping for, the advent of Katherine Loring[2] in 2 or 3 weeks.—My disappointment at missing that little snatch of Venice still keeps its edge—such edge, at least, as was not, I frankly confess, taken off, on Sunday last, by the rather sickening heat which I encountered on descending from Vallombrosa to Florence. I stand that sort of temperature badly & at the moment it half consoled me. But I hope Venice is a trifle fresher, the Barbaro not absolutely unconscious of a breeze & your mosquito-curtains (I won't say thick but) of an impenetrable gossamer. Heaven forbid I should be absent from London when you come. I shall make no long absence till I go to Paris (if I do go,) late in the autumn. And that won't be very long, only kindly let me have a word as you approach. Please give my love & all my regrets to Mrs. Bronson[3]—tell her I love her, but feel how little circumstances smile on our union. (She will explain this to you.)—And may I further impose on your gracious good nature so far as to ask you very benevolently just to *mention* to Angelo that some people (from the forwarding agents) will call for the trunk I left at the Barbaro on July 1*st*—not wanting to travel further with it & cherishing a private vision that you would ask me to come back in August. Much good did my little combination do me! But *pazienza.* Kindly repeat my regrets to your husband & believe me most truly yours

Henry James

NOTES

1 Alice James had taken a house in Leamington in 1889, with a nurse. Katherine Loring had gone back to America; see Strouse p 296.

2 See letter 22, note 4. The relation between Alice James and Katherine Loring was very intense, with bouts of jealousy on Alice's part when Katherine dedicated herself to her own invalid sister Louisa.

3 See letter 27, note 5. James may be alluding to some inscrutable gossiping.

XLVII

(Ms I S G M)

34, De Vere Gardens, W. Tuesday a.m.[1]

Dear Mrs. Gardner.
Welcome to "town!" I will come in with great pleasure at 5 p.m. to-day. Alice is really better, thanks largely to a change of habitat.[2] She is at present in London for a few months. Ever yours

Henry James

NOTES

1 Probably 1890.

2 James's sister Alice had moved to the South Kensington Hotel, in London, on 2nd September 1890, with Katherine Loring, not far from Henry James.

XLVIII

(Ms I S G M)

34, De Vere Gardens, W. *Sept. 30th* [1890]

Dear Mrs. Gardner—

I find I was mistaken by ½ an hour about the train to Hever:[1] it leaves Victoria at 2.35 & gets to Hever at a quarter to 4. But this would give us an hour there, as the castle is only a mile from the station, & an hour is all we shd., in any case, use—more in fact. We shall, I fear, have a little time on our hands before a return train—but perhaps we can potter about or get rid of that by driving to some other station (Edenbridge) whence there may be an earlier train. There is one, I see, from Edenbridge—5.20. Therefore I shall be at Victoria (*London & Brighton Line*) by or before 2.25, eagerly looking out for you. A démain. Ever yours

Henry James

NOTE

1 Beautiful Hever Castle, near Edenbridge, Kent, where Anne Boleyn lived as a child. The castle, built in the thirteenth century, was enlarged in the sixteenth century by the Boleyns; it then became the property of Anne of Clèves, wife of Henry VIII, and had several owners from 1557 onwards. In 1903 it was bought by William Waldorf Astor, who restored it and also built a Tudor village and a garden on formerly marshy lands. A magnificent *Book of Hours* of Anne Boleyn's is still preserved in the castle. This is one of the visits that may have inspired Mrs Gardner to make her own museum.

XLIX

(Ms I S G M, Edel)

34, De Vere Gardens, W. June 7th [1891]

My dear Mrs. Gardner.
You always do graceful & generous things promptly & swiftly, & I always thank you for them a hundred years too late. Don't deny it—your magnanimity is capable even of that—for the present is a crowning proof. Your sympathetic word about my poor little play[1] went to my heart when it came—& it has lain locked up there ever since. I pull it out, with a violent effort, to turn it over & handle it a little again—but the frowning portals of that organ gape wide for me to put it quickly back among the slumbering echoes & dried roseleaves.

There it goes—don't you hear the click of the lock? I wish indeed I were going to America to "produce" my dramatic production—for heaven knows how that ticklish business will go off when the time comes. The time will not come till it has been a *London* success—if success it is to be. I have refused the most glittering American offers in order to elicit still more glittering ones on the basis of a triumph in *this* place. The thing has only been acted as yet in the provinces—but I am happy to say its success in the big cities (the bigger the place the better it goes,) constitutes a basis for hope. Meanwhile London doesn't see it till the 26*th* September next—when one *does* hope that it will run all winter. These are rash words to utter—so please kindly scratch them out yourself—to make sure. The piece is really very well cast, as things go on the *scène anglaise* for town, & I am to have really quite adorable scenery—which it has been very amusing to go into the gorgeous details of—A young American actress[2] who never made a mark, I believe, *chez vous*, has lately revealed herself, strikingly, here, as Ibsen's *Hedda Gabler*, & has quite leaped into fame. She is slightly uncanny, but distinguished & individual, & she is to do my heroine; a short part, but a very pretty one.—It's a bad business that you don't come out this summer, for I shouldn't miss you by going to Italy. If it didn't sound vainglorious I should add that neither would you, by going there—miss me. However, perhaps you would go all the same—I only meant that I fear there are, this year, no loose palaces knocking about. The Curtises go to India[3]—or believe they do—in the autumn; so I suppose they summerize at the Barbaro. Happy thought—you come out in the autumn & occupy the Barbaro during their absence & give me then a lease of their top-floor. *They* won't—so this is my only way to get it. This is a pale, dim, cold, skeptical season—a season that doesn't believe in itself. It's a thousand pities you are *not* here to stimulate its credulity. My sister has a very nice house to be very ill in[4]—& it isn't a waste. Katherine Loring is, still, the very foundation of our Universe. I hope *yours*, dear Mrs. Gardner, keeps in tolerable repair—your Universe I mean. But everything of yours is always in lovely order—except indeed a thing so very & peculiarly & intensely yours, as

Henry James

NOTES

1 The play *The American* was premiered at Southport, near Liverpool, on 3rd January 1891, and James was present; it was, according to Alice James, "as far as audience, Compton (the company) and author were concerned, a brilliant success" Edel *Diary of Alice James* p 161. The London premiere was on 26th September 1891, at the Opera Comique, and ran for five weeks; see letter to Stevenson, 30th October 1891, *Selected Letters* p 247. It "died an honourable death, on the 76th night", as Alice James wrote in her diary on 30th December 1891 (*Diary* p 224). See also Edel *Complete Plays* pp 179–91.

2 The American actress was Kentucky-born Elizabeth Robins (1863–1952). James met her in January 1891, seeing her in Ibsen's *A Doll's House* (Robins p 25). He greatly admired her in *Hedda Gabler.* James wrote on Ibsen in June 1891, *Henrik Ibsen: On the Occasion of Hedda Gabler*; reprinted as the first part of the Ibsen essay in *Essays in London and Elsewhere* (1893). James was more enthusiastic seeing Ibsen on the stage than in reading him. Miss Robins played the part of Madame de Cintré in the London production of *The American*; see *Notebooks* p 203 n 3. After retiring from the stage, Miss Robins went in "for literature, Female Suffrage, the Colour Question in the US (she springs from Louisville, Ky) and various other activities", as Henry James wrote to his brother on 13th November 1907 (*The Correspondence of William James, William and Henry* III p 352). The book on the Colour Question was apparently never done.

3 The Curtises did go to India in 1893–94.

4 Alice and Katherine had moved to 41 Argyll Road, Kensington, W, on 12th March 1891.

L

(Ms I S G M)

34, De Vere Gardens, W.[1] *April 15th* [1892]

Dear Mrs. Gardner—
Welcome back to the ancient world[2] which your presence makes a little younger for the hour. I say this, alas, very disinterestedly, for I fear I shant be in London when you gracefully alight upon it. I have been awaiting you here for the last ten months & my health has broken down under the quantity of hope deferred.—Seriously speaking I go away, a week or two hence, for the season, but I don't even yet figure to myself where I go.—I see the news has not reached you of my sister's death which occurred on the 6*th* March & as a sequel to which K.P.L.[3] sailed from Liverpool on Saturday last. That long, sad chapter is over—& I have been through a series of melancholy weeks.—Somewhere, somehow, however, surely we shall meet. I may not even go abroad—but only to some remote & inaccessible part of these islands. On the other hand I *may* betake myself to some impenetrable corner of

Italy. Everything is yet in the vague. My brother[4] & his wife & children come out (to the continent,) early in June[5]—& I shall meet them in Switzerland. Shan't I also meet you? I hope Paris speaks to you still, & says civil things. It's a comfort to know you are one of the possibilities of the hour & to feel that I am always your devotissimo

Henry James

NOTES

1 The writing paper has black edges, as do letters 51 and 52, for Alice's death.

2 On 2nd April 1892, the Gardners left for Europe. They went to Paris, London and Venice, staying at Palazzo Barbaro (arriving 14th June) and leaving in August to go to Switzerland, Dresden, Munich, then coming back to Venice at the end of August, and again in Paris, from 22nd September till December. See Mrs Gardner *Scrapbook* n 12.

3 Katherine Peabody Loring.

4 William, with his wife Alice Howe Gibbens (1849–1922) and their children Henry (1879–1947), William (1882–1961), Margaret (Peggy) (1887–1950) and Alexander Roberston (1890–1946). Herman, born in 1884, died at eighteen months, in 1885.

5 The William James family sailed from New York on the *Friesland* on 25th May. They spent more than a year in Europe, staying in Florence through March 1893. William went to Padua, "to transact some psychical research" (*The Correspondence of William James, William and Henry* II p 240) and to Venice in November. The family then went to Switzerland (April 1893) and England, leaving from Liverpool on 24th August 1893, and arriving in Boston on 2nd September.

LI

(Ms I S G M)

34, De Vere Gardens, W. April 19th [1892]

Dear Mrs. Gardner.
Your kind note breathes a spirit of hospitality, which I gratefully appreciate. I am afraid it is a little early for me to [be] able to say, definitely, what I may hope to be able to do in regard to Venice—I don't yet see the form of my summer & have several possibilities to reckon with. But it is delightful to think of paying you a little visit[1] (what delightful fates & fortunes you have!) & I shall from this moment cherish the vision & work—to my utmost—towards it. I may perhaps dream of it more lucidly for June-July than for the 2d period—& yet I don't know. It is a charming open door—into bliss. I fly from this place—for parts unknown—as soon as I can. I will write you a more definite word the 1st moment I see more clearly. Yours always

Henry James

NOTE

1 James eventually went to Venice, to the Palazzo Barbaro, after spending a month in Tuscany. He arrived in Venice on 8th July and left for Switzerland on 24th July, to meet his brother William and his family.

LII

(Ms I S G M)

Hotel de Sienne. *Siena.* June 26th [1892]

My dear Mrs. Gardner.
Many thanks for your little paper-light[1] of a letter. I have had 50 thoughts of writing to you, but have waited, inevitably, till it should seem I was seeing a little more clearly into the question of my getting next month to Venice. I am not very lucid about it yet. I have only a general passionate tendency toward it—i.e. toward the Barbaro. The truth is I am utterly bewildered & distraught by conflicting & maddening appeals to me from different people to come to different places. I came to Italy to *hide*—but I don't succeed.

Is it, by chance, my glory? That seems to me hardly sufficient to account for it. At all events it is my curse, & I am bowed down under it. Therefore I cling from day to day to this sweet old Siena, which *isn't* a "different place"—from what it is. There were days when I went up to the great campanile & looked out for you, Bourget[2] stood at the bottom & cried "Sister

Anne, do you see her?"[3] You ought to have come. The spell of Siena is upon me—it suits me to perfection. It's awfully hot, but cooler, I ween, than Torcello! I have a big cool saloon in which I stay almost all day—till 6—when I go into the world. I live in harmony with the Bourgets who had a house at 1*st*—but have come back to the hotel, where they have another big dim saloon in which *they* sit all day—till 6. That's how we manage not to quarrel. But we breakfast & dine together & walk on the Lizza & eat 6 ices apiece every evening at the café. We are as *spirituel* as we can be—& just now we have Giuseppe Primoli[4]—of Rome—an odd little member of the Bonaparte family, who completes the brilliancy of our group. M*me* P.B. is very young, very lovely & very clever. All the same I greatly hope to get off on July 5*th*—*about.* You shall have the earliest definite word—since you are so good as to ask me—about my approach to Venice. It would be affectation to pretend that I delight in excursions—or in any long confinement in a moving vehicle, by land or sea. But I do delight in everything Venetian—I have a weakness even for the vaporetti. Tell it not to the Curtises.[5] Is Mrs. Mason[6] in Venice still? Will you give her please, my friendliest greeting. I shall write you again at the end of the week—& am ever, dear Mrs. Gardner, your devotissimo

Henry James

NOTES

1 'Paper-light', in contrast to 'paper-weight'.

2 Paul Bourget (1852–1935), French writer, introduced to James by Sargent in 1884. He married Minnie David (c 1868–1932) in 1890. After his Italian honeymoon he published *Sensations d'Italie* (1891). Well known as a critic and a psychological novelist, he wrote many novels from 1874, among which are *Cruelle Enigme* (1885) and *Le Disciple* (1888). *Cosmopolis* (1892), his best-known novel, portrays the international society in which he lived. James introduced the Bourgets to Mrs Gardner, when they went to America (see letter 57), see Wrenn.

3 An allusion to the story of Bluebeard, where his last wife, doomed to die, asks to pray for a quarter-of-an-hour while her sister Anne climbs the tower to see if their brothers are arriving. The question, 'Anne, sister Anne, do you see anyone coming?', is sometimes used in literary texts.

4 Count Giuseppe Primoli (1851–1927) grew up in Paris and went to Rome in 1870. He was a prominent figure in the Roman intellectual circles of the end of the century; a bibliophile, and above all a photographer quite well known for his portraits of famous people, he also staged many *tableaux vivants*. He descended, through his mother, Charlotte Bonaparte, from Charles Lucien, prince of Canino, son of Luciano Bonaparte, Napoleon's brother. On Saturday 9th February 1895, the Gardners attended a magic lantern soirée at Primoli's (John L Gardner *Travel Diaries* 1895).

5 Daniel Sargent Curtis (1825–1908) and his wife Ariana Wormeley Curtis (1833–1922), the owners, from 1885, of the

magnificent Palazzo Barbaro on the Grand Canal, which Mrs Gardner rented more than once from 1890, and which gave her the inspiration for the Venetian façades in the courtyard of Fenway Court.

6 For Mrs Mason, see letters 3 and 98.

LIII

(Ms I S G M)

Hotel de Sienne *Thursday* [1892]

Dear Mrs. Gardner—
Many renewed thanks. Please judge me leniently when I say that my circumstances make it difficult for me to pronounce very definitely as to *dates.* They are terrible things—when one is burrowing in holes—& one of the things that I fled from London—where one lives calendar in hand—to escape. But I have a very fond hope of reaching Venice on the *10th*. In this case—in *any* case—I will let you know with absolute definiteness 3 or 4 days beforehand. The uncertain quantity in the matter is largely the heat, which makes me rather sick, & terribly timorous about tying myself. Is Asolo[1] *cool?*—I have a shrewd suspicion that it's a sociable Tophet[2]—a suspicion confirmed by the presence there of Don Mephistopheles.[3] Will you however please say to our good friend[4]—with my tender love—that if I can hold up my head at all I will make every effort to accompany you there on the 16*th*. I am not, like her,

a salamander,[5] or like you a block of fine marble—& I *may* liquefy in the meanwhile. But there is safety for me in M*me* P.B.'s[6] coolness to me—that may hold me together. I have complications for next week—which make me venture to mention no day *earlier* than the 10*th*.[7] But if I can manage one I will strain every nerve to do so. Yours, dear Mrs. Gardner, always

Henry James

NOTES

1 Asolo basically meant Mrs Bronson's house 'La Mura', where the members of the Anglo-American community of Venice and Florence often met.

2 'Tophet', as a hellishly hot place. In another letter James called Mrs Bronson's Asolo house a "glasshouse".

3 Maybe James is referring to Don Carlos of Bourbon (1848–1909), the pretender to the throne of Spain, and a member of the international expatriate community of Venice. He lived in the Palazzo Loredan. Years later, in his letters to Norwegian-American sculptor Hendrik Andersen, James called the painter Gustavo Bacarisas "Mephistopheles". Bacarisas does have a Mephistophelian look in the photographs; see *Beloved Boy* p 70.

4 Mrs Bronson, at 'La Mura'.

5 James suffered a lot from the heat. He also used the metaphor of the salamander for those who loved the heat in a letter to Hendrik Andersen: "you are all salamanders by now, clearly—or you would long since have yielded to the forces of perspiration" (3rd August 1909 *Beloved Boy* p 90).

6 Madame Paul Bourget.

7 James in fact arrived in Venice from Bologna "abt 2 p.m.", on Thursday, 7th July, as Mr Gardner annotated in his diary.

LIV

(Ms I S G M, Edel)

Hotel Richemont
Lausanne
Friday (July 29th) [1892]

Dear Donna Isabella—
I have waited to draw breath here before writing to you—& I arrived here only yesterday. Italy is already a dream & Venice a superstition. The Barbaro is a phantom & Donna Isabella herself but an exquisite legend. You all melt away in this hard Swiss light. But I have just bought a tinted (I believe they call it a "smoked" pince-nez,) & I am attempting to focus you again. I carried my bleeding heart, last Sunday, all the way to Turin; where I literally spent two days (the Hotel de l'Europe there is excellent,) & finished the abominable article.[1]

With that atrocity on my conscience I deserved nothing better, doubtless, than the melancholy Mont Cenis, which dragged me last Wednesday, through torrid heats, straight out of Paradise, fighting every inch of the way. Switzerland is much hotter than Italy, &, for beauty, not to be mentioned in the same cycle of time. It's a pleasantry to say it has charm. I have been here (in this particular desolation,) since yesterday noon, intensely occupied in realizing that I am an uncle.[2] It is very serious—but I am fully taking it in. I don't see, as yet, how long I shall remain one—but sufficient unto the day are the nephews thereof. Mine, here, are domiciled with pastori in the neighbouring valleys, but are let loose in honour of my arrival. They are charming & the little girl a *bellezza*. My brother & his wife send you the friendliest greetings & thank you for all you have done—& are doing—for me. My windows from this high hillside, hang over the big lake & sweep it from one end to the other, but the view isn't comparable to that of the little canal-end from the divine library[3] of the Barbaro. I am utterly homesick for Venice. Il n'y a que ça.—Our smash[4] on the way to the station is almost an agreeable recollection to me—simply for being so Venetian. Gardner will have told you all about it, but I hope there have been no tiresome sequels. I don't know, but I *think* it arose from a want of competence on the part of the fallible Domenico, who had the prow-oars I shall be eager to hear from you some day ce que s'en suivi. I am hungry for Venetian & Asolan gossip. I want to know everything you have bought[5] these last days—even for yourself. Or has *everything* been for me? I pray this may catch you before you start for this cruel country. I enclose the introducing word for Lady Brooke,[6] to whom I am also writing. My station here is precarious, as my brother, I believe, thinks of going somewhere else—so I don't venture to ask you to write any where but to De Vere Gardens (34)—if you are so charitable as to write—or if you ever *can* write again after the handkissing extraordinary[7] that I ween the Barbaro will witness on Monday. Please give my friendliest remembrance to Gardner, whom I thank afresh for his company and protection last Sunday a.m.—how long ago and far-away it seems! If he hadn't been there to steady the boat, Domenico would probably have sent me to the bottom. I am more & more determined however, in spite of such perils, to secure a Venetian home. I largely depend upon you for it, & I am, dear, generous lady, your devotissimo

Henry James

NOTES

1 The essay *The Grand Canal*, published in *Scribner's Magazine* (xii November 1892), and collected in *Italian Hours* (1909). The magazine editor, E L Burlingame, had sent the illustrations by painter Alessandro Zezzos to James, but, according to James, these had not helped him at all in writing the essay, on the contrary. James wrote to Burlingame: "In truth I can't write for illustration. I am too greedily jealous for my own prose", (Edel *Letters III* p 393).

2 James went from Venice to Switzerland to meet his brother William and his wife, and their four children. He spent about ten days there, but was disappointed as William left for a tour of the Engadine soon after he had arrived (see letter 55).

3 James alludes to the magnificent library on the top floor of the Palazzo Barbaro, where Mrs Gardner placed a four-poster bed, with a mosquito net, for James, as the whole apartment was full of guests. James loved sleeping in the "divine old library", which allowed him to admire the ceiling stucco work and medallions, as he wrote to Ariana Curtis; see *Letters from the Palazzo Barbaro* p 121.

4 Mr Gardner wrote in his diary on Sunday, 24th July 1892: "H James left by 9 am train for Geneva via Turin. Went to Station with him. Collision with another boat going round a corner" (*Travel Diaries* 1892).

5 Simply looking at the meagre entries in Jack Gardner's diary, one sees the intensity of Mr and Mrs Gardner's visits to antiques dealers: in Venice, on 25th July, for instance, they went to "Guggenheim, Besarel, Dalla Torre and Clerlé" in the

morning, and to "Carrer and Dalla Torre" in the afternoon (*Travel Diaries* 1892).

6 Lady Margaret Alice de Windt Brooke (1849–1936), married the second raja of Sarawak, becoming Ranee of Sarawak. She was a friend of Henry James, a beautiful woman and a gifted pianist. She went to Sarawak in 1870 with her husband, and had three children there, who all died of cholera on the return voyage in 1873. She had three more sons. From the mid-1880s the couple led separate lives. She visited Sarawak for the last time in 1895. See Bob Reece *The White Rajas of Sarawak. A Borneo Dynasty* Singapore Archipelago Press 2004 pp 59–64.

7 James might be alluding here to a visit to Palazzo Barbaro by the Duke and the Duchess of Genoa, who were in town in those days. They attended a special serenade on the Grand Canal, where Pier Adolfo Tirindelli, a musician, and a great friend of Mrs Gardner's, participated. On Monday 1st August, "*alle 4, in gondola di lusso, i duchi di Genova assieme al Sindaco percorsero il Canalazzo circondati dalle bissone e dai solazzieri, e dalla folla salutati con applausi*" [at four o'clock, in a luxury gondola, the Dukes of Genoa, together with the Mayor, floated along the Grand Canal, surrounded by decorated barges and rowing boats, and applauded by the crowd]. They were going to Ca' Foscari, where the Duchess appeared on the balcony to hail the crowds. In another gondola followed "*il principino Ferdinando col suo precettore*" [young Prince Ferdinand with his tutor]. (*La Gazzetta di Venezia* 1st August 1982). On 3rd August the Duchess gave out prizes to the girls of the Collegio Giustinian (ibid 4th August).

LV

(Ms I S G M, Lubbock)

34 De Vere Gdns. W. *Sept. 3ᵈ* [1892]

Dear Donna Isabel.
I don't know where this will find you, but I hope it will find you with your hair not quite "up"—neither up nor down, as it were, in a gauze dressing-gown, on a seagreen (so different from peagreen!) chair, beneath a glorious gilded ceiling, receiving the matutinal tea from a Venetian slave. I never answered the delightful letter you were so good as to write me on the eve of your departure from Venice because I thought it only fair to leave you alone a month—to reward, in a word, by an effort of abnegation, the patience with which, during so many weeks, you harmonized our conflicting claims. Now, however, that you have fallen back into your incorrigible hospitalities you expose yourself to the outrage of friendship & I have—comparatively speaking—no scruple in peeping into your dim saloon.[1] Don't tell me that you are *not* seated there in the attitude & costume which it was apparently my sole privilege

to admire—I mean only *my* not my *only* privilege. I am haunted by vague apprehensions that you may be fidgeted by visions of cholera & quarantine[2]—begotten indeed by the solitary, foolish little circumstance that an American youth (Richard Norton)[3] whom I was thinking of "sending" to you & who was at any rate to spend September in Venice, writes me that he has given it up at the behest of "the doctors." He was a fool to *ask* the doctors—one would know what they would say. I hope you have done nothing of the kind, & indeed I don't see you. Therefore if the interlude is over your light tread is again on the marble floors. I wish I could patter along that polished perspective of the library[4] again. I would give all the tin watering-pots I possess to see the big Tita come in, in the morning, on diffident tiptoe, with my bath in a coffee-vessel. I should like greatly to hear your late adventures, and all about the Engadine & Bayreuth and the rest. Did you go to Vienna? I hope not—to be cooked over, like something underdone, which you surely are not. Did Bayreuth come off, & did the Ranee[5] come on?—My own history has been mortally dull. After romance the sternest realities. I spent a fortnight near my brother on the Lake of Geneva—as "near" as was possible to a brother who started for Engadine & Chamounix as soon as I arrived—the inevitable reward of a virtuous sacrifice. *N'en faites jamais!* If it was to be done over—how I would have waited for the regatta![6]

Delightful was your picture of this scene with the casual recompense of Mrs. Mason's gondolier. I can see the gesture with which she shied it at him! But I wish I had been there to see all the rest!—Do tell me how the dear old place looks & feels—only not how it smells—again! Are the little white papers on *my* clean shutters still? Probably not—& my pink chairs & my lemon sofa have also been snatched up. But tell me what chances survive—what *occasions* await. I haven't seen the Curtises yet—they are still in Norfolk.[7] But I believe they come up from one day to another. I am supposed to be at Brighton, but I came back yesterday under stress of deplorable weather! I am in & out, but I have my eye on the proprietors of the topmost floor. Tell me something about Asolo and the unspeakable Goldona.[8] Do go down there; take a drive—& a walk—& a sit for me—Tell me about the court at teatime & if there is any *jeunesse* left to come to it. My brother & his wife & children spend the winter in Florence & I fear I can't go to Italy again till I go to see them. But I shall go as soon as I can.

I shall, however, take intense pains to be here when you come.—Is the little Smith[9] still in the field? Give my love to him if he is. I send *tanti saluti* to the padrone, & am, dear Donna Isabel, ever the padrona's devotissimo

Henry James

NOTES

1 The wonderful *salon* of the Palazzo Barbaro, built by architect Antonio Gaspari at the end of the seventeenth century, and decorated with stuccowork and paintings by Piazzetta, Ricci, Balestra, Zanchi and Tiepolo. See *Letters from the Palazzo Barbaro* p 49.

2 Cholera was periodically announced and declared non-existent by the newspapers, as, for instance, in the summer of 1892, in the *Gazzetta di Venezia.* The Gardners changed hotel in 1886 because of a case of cholera where they were staying, the Hotel de l'Europe (*Travel Diaries 1886* p 5).

3 Richard Norton (1872–1918), son of Charles Eliot Norton, the future archaeologist and director of the School of Classic Studies in Rome. He died of meningitis in Paris.

4 The library of the Palazzo Barbaro; see letter 54.

5 See letter 54, note 6.

6 The regatta along the Grand Canal takes place on the first Sunday in September.

7 To see their son Osborne.

8 Goldona—probably an allusion to Mrs Bronson's Goldoni-like plays in Venetian.

James often created Italian-sounding nicknames, such as "Pamperina" for Lady Kenmare, "Whartonina" for Edith Wharton and "Sacramentina" for Mrs Howells, all using the diminutive Italian form.

9 Joseph Lindon Smith (1863–1950), the American painter whom Mrs Gardner met while he was on top of a scaffolding, on the monument to Bartolomeo Colleoni, in Campo SS Giovanni and Paolo, in Venice. Smith was painting a portrait

of Colleoni's face. The portrait caused him to be nicknamed "Colle". Apparently Mrs Gardner asked to climb to the top too. After being a guest of Edward Robinson at Palazzo Dario, in September Smith moved to the Palazzo Barbaro as one of Mrs Gardner's court of young artists. She bought five Venetian watercolours by Smith, and it was Smith who procured the *Hercules* by Piero della Francesca for Mrs Gardner. Before she died, Mrs Gardner asked Smith to direct the Fenway Court museum, but he refused. See Chong *Gondola Days* pp 160–61.

LVI

(Ms I S G M)

Hotel Westminster[1]
Paris. May 1st 1893.

Dearest lady & old kind friend.
You don't know to what a tune your gentle letter is a balm to my spirit. For it re-establishes a communication too long & too ungracefully interrupted—& interrupted, as I have felt for months, by my own failures and lapses. I think I wrote to you—I mean *had* written to you, last; but cela ne fait rien à l'affaire. Your showers of hospitality and bounty last summer—the ineffaceable vision of those adored Venetian days—have left me permanently in your debt. Therefore whenever I don't write to you—or do *something* to you—I am *wrong*, and I distinctly admit it, once for all. But I *am* writing to you now; & the only hitch in the matter is that after all it seems somehow too pleasant to be *right*! The revolving year brings me round my inevitable Venice-hunger—and yet there is little prospect of my even "staying" my stomach. I have been these 7 weeks in Paris—&

I go to-morrow to Lucerne, to join my brother & his wife,[2] who just arrive from Florence, where they have wintered. But further on the way I can't move, as they are coming to England on June 1*st* & I must be there to be hospitable. It is no pleasure to me to cross the Alps for the scrap of time between. Paris has been incomparably bright and warm—with its share of the radiant drought[3] which has hung for many, many weeks over all Europe & the fame of which has reached, probably, even your rainless (comparatively) clime. I believe all growing things are refusing to grow—but Paris has been lovely. I have tried to be quiet here—but I have utterly failed—you have seen, for yourself, how utterly I *do* fail. I went to tea yesterday with the Whistlers[4] in their green little garden-house of the rue du Bac, where the only furniture is the paint on the walls and the smile on the lady's broad face. We had, however, tea & cakes & Cushings.[5] I *don't* mean cushions—though you might think it. I have seen a good deal of my dear old friend Miss Reubell[6]—for whom my affection glows with a steady flame. She tells me she has strange ravings from Mrs. Crafts[7] (lately arrived here,) over the Boston-beauty of your wondrous masquerade[8]—at which the gentlemen revealed unsuspected, or hitherto unappreciated *legs*. And what did the ladies reveal? Some of them will have had hard work to make manifest anything not hitherto much appreciated. You are wonderful people and the evident *cinque-centisti* of the future. What calculated torture, on your part, not telling me what you were to wear! I am however too lost in visions to trouble much—visions of what you will invent to make up next year for not having come to Europe *this* one. Count upon me to assist you in realizing it. I figure you somehow—strange as is the association of ideas—at the remarkable Chicago[9]—with a "building"—an infinitely more barbarous Barbaro—all to yourself. Won't there be the Federal buildings, & the States buildings, and then, in a category by itself, Mrs. Jack's building? I wish I could have a little marble hall at the top of it, with 13 screens and a pink mosquito-netting[10]—On these terms will I come—on none others. I can't tell you how shocked I am to hear of the dreadful death of that poor little younger Smith.[11] I think of the poor father & mother & their so charming united family life. To have had that golden summer in Venice—& then to have *that*—& go home for it! How strange & horrible is life. Please say something *very* kind for me to that good elder boy. I hope he has a firm & safe refuge in his great talent. How I remember *everything* of last July! Best, perhaps, the little evening-journey—so romantic, so Italian, the night we went to Asolo. Have you seen the robust but restrained Collins[12] again—& what is he doing? Tell him, if you meet him, that I wish he were smoking a cigarette *en face de ma table de travail*—as he used to do at the Barbaro. Continue to live—dearest lady—and to enhance & refresh, by the balmy breeze that vital motion of yours creates, the more torpid contemporary existence of yours ever most affectionately

Henry James

NOTES

1 Written by hand.

2 See letter 50, also for their departure from England.

3 William James also mentioned the drought in a letter from Meggen, near Lucerne, of 24th April: "The drouth hasn't sensibly affected the vegetation and the hill sides are a carpet of fruit trees in blossom—the finest bloom known in 40 years they say" (*The Correspondence of William James, William and Henry* II p 267).

4 James Abbott McNeill Whistler (1834–1903), American painter, and his wife Beatrix Philip (1857–96), an artist. After living together, they were married in 1888, when her first husband died. She died of cancer. James had met Whistler in the 1870s, and Isabella had met him in London in 1879 and saw him and Beatrix in Paris during her various visits. James, strangely for such an innovator in narrative, did not appreciate Whistler initially: "a picture should have some relation to life as well as to painting. Mr Whistler's experiments have no relation whatever to life; they have only a relation to painting" (*Painter's Eye* 1877 p 143). Whistler's paintings were "so very eccentric and imperfect" (*Painter's Eye* 1878 p 174). James instead admired greatly his etchings and eventually also came to like his paintings, such as *Arrangement in Black No 3*, in the 1890s (*Painter's Eye Introduction* p 26). See also *Whistler.*

In his essay of 1878 on the Ruskin–Whistler controversy, James did not really support one or the other. Whistler had taken Ruskin to court over his words on Whistler's abstract *Nocturnes* exhibited at the Grosvenor Gallery in 1877: "I have seen and heard much of cockney impudence before now; but never expected to hear a coxcomb ask 200 guineas for flinging a pot of paint in the public's face" (*Painter's Eye* p 172). (Whistler won, but was ruined by the expenses; he was given a stipend to go to Venice, where he stayed longer than planned, in 1879–80, creating a famous series of etchings and pastels, later exhibited in London.)

In 1886 Mrs Gardner bought some Whistler pastels in London, including *The Little Note in Yellow and Gold* (a portrait of herself), but no Venetian scenes, while in June 1889 she bought four etchings, among which were the Venetian subjects *San Biagio* and *Little Venice*; in 1890, at New York, she finally bought the two complete series of the Venetian etchings of 1880 and 1886. In 1892, in Paris, Mrs Gardner bought *Harmony in Blue and Silver* (Tharp p 167, Denker p 11 and McCauley *Gondola Days* p 15 e 46). On 21st September 1897, Violet Paget wrote to Mrs Gardner asking her to buy some paintings from the 'peacock' room, decorated by Whistler against his patron F Leyland's directions in 1876. Other artists, such as Sargent (letter of August 29th, 1893 or 1895 Whistler correspondence Isabella Stewart Gardner Museum), wrote to her about this possibility. Mrs Gardner apparently did not buy them (Letter, BNM, Whistler correspondence). The Peacock Room paintings were finally bought by Charles Lang Freer. *Eye of the Beholder* p 196. Whistler's garden in Rue du Bac was the 'germ' for Gloriani's garden in *The Ambassadors* (1903).

5 Probably the American painter Howard Cushing (1869–1916), of an aristocratic Boston family, who studied at the Académie Julien in Paris 1891–96, and married Ethel Cochrane in 1904;

Mrs Gardner annotated in her diary of 19th December 1892, that she had seen Howard Cushing, and perhaps also his older brother, Grafton, a lawyer, and/or their parents. Grafton Dulany Cushing (1864–1936) was a guest of the Gardners in Boston in June 1897. See *Guestbook 1897–99*. One of Howard's and Grafton's sisters was Olivia, who married Andreas Andersen, the brother of sculptor Hendrik Andersen, whom Henry James met in Rome and fell in love with in 1899. Andreas Andersen was a guest at Green Hill in 1898. Olivia, widowed a month after her marriage (1902), decided to spend the rest of her life in Rome, with Hendrik Andersen and his mother; see *Beloved Boy*.

6 Henrietta Reubell (c 1848–49–post 1904), whom James met in Paris in 1876, his great friend and correspondent (James wrote more than a hundred letters to her). "*La grande demoiselle*", as James called her, was an American expatriate living in Paris, of a partly French family; she had a salon frequented by artists and painters. The character of Miss Barrace in *The Ambassadors* was in part inspired by her. Sargent painted her portrait in 1884–85: many of James's letters to her have comments on Sargent's paintings. See Ormond-Kilmurray *The Early Portraits* p 154.

7 Clémence Haggerty Crafts (1841–1912) was the wife of a famous chemist at The Massachusetts Institute of Technology, James Mason Crafts (1839–1917); they had four daughters. They lived at 57 Marlborough Street, and from 1907 at 111 Commonwealth, in Boston, while they had a summer place at Ridgefield, Connecticut.

8 A few years earlier (1889), Mrs Gardner had participated in a masked charity ball for young artists, dressing as a

Veronese lady, with a little blackamoor holding her train. She was portrayed in this pink damask gown by Dennis Miller Bunker (Isabella Stewart Gardner Museum); see Mamoli Zorzi 2002 pp 63–66. See also letters 43 and 64.

9 The Gardners lent a painting to the 1893 Chicago World Columbian Exposition and were invited to go before the opening. It was there that Mrs Gardner saw Anders Zorn's painting *The Omnibus*, bought it, met the Zorns and later invited them to Venice. The exposition had more than 200 buildings, representing the government and the various states. There were also a Transportation Building, a Fine Arts Building, a Woman's Building, a Horticultural Building, a Machinery building and foreign and ethnographic buildings.

10 James is humorously hinting at his bed in the library on the top floor of Palazzo Barbaro, in1892, when he was a guest of Mrs Gardner's. See letter 54, note 3.

11 The death of Joseph Lindon Smith's younger brother, who had been in Venice with his parents the previous summer.

12 Alfred Q Collins (1855–1903), American painter. Coming from a poor Boston family, he was sent to study art in Paris by Quincy Shaw. He is described by John Jay Chapman in his *Memories and Milestones* as follows: "Collins had a chiseled brow, a straight nose and blazing eyes and was extraordinarily handsome before he became heavy", and he was "of a powerful build, he knew how to box … and he loved feats of strength in the studio" (Chapman p 262). He became a member of the American Academy of Arts and Letters in 1898.

LVII

(Ms I S G M)

34, De Vere Gardens, W. August 4th *1893*

Dear Mrs. Gardner.
Please offer that very generous hand of yours to my distinguished & charming friends Paul Bourget & Madame Paul Bourget,[1] as to whom I shall not in the least, in these three words of confident instruction, endeavour to attenuate the circumstance that they *count* upon you—at my instigation—to project upon the Boston of their admirably intelligent curiosity the light of your hospitality, of your grace, of your exquisite energy & even of your indulgent friendship for yours, dear Mrs. Gardner, always devotedly

Henry James

P. S. I particularly want them to meet our incomparable Wendell Holmes the younger[2]—the eternally youngest; and I cannot better act in the spirit of the affection I bear him than by placing this happy privilege for him under auspices that he will appreciate as much as he must always appreciate every office of yours.

H.J.

NOTES

1 See letter 52, note 2. After passing through New York, the Bourgets went to Newport in August, to Boston by yacht in September, and then to the World Fair in Chicago. The *Boston Globe* of 5th September had a long article, on their arrival in Boston from Newport, their being guests of Mrs Gardner at Beverly, and Bourget's impressions of the Labour Day Parade in Boston and of Newport. On other dates it quoted excerpts from Bourget's work, his comments on the art knowledge of American women and his impressions of the Chicago Fair: "Paul Bourget is enchanted with the World's Fair. It is not, however, so cosmopolitan as was the Paris exposition, he says" (27th September 1893). From the American trip was born *Outre-Mer* (1894), where Bourget described Mrs Gardner's portrait by Sargent.

2 Oliver Wendell Holmes, Jr (1841–1935), jurist, son of Oliver Wendell Holmes (1809–94), and famous above all for his *Autocrat at the Breakfast Table.* Bourget met him on the occasion of the elder Holmes's eighty-fourth birthday celebrations at Beverly; see Tharp p 170.

LVIII

(Ms I S G M)

43, De Vere Gardens, W. August 5th *1893*

Dear Mrs. Gardner.

Paul Bourget & his quite exceptional young wife sail for America today (c/o August Belmont Co., bankers, New York,) & I have had the reckless courage to give them a note of introduction to you. My next duty is to confess to you my misdemeanour. I do so the more promptly that I am sure you will condone it when they turn up. They will be very vague & helpless & hot, at first, I fear, but if they enter into communication with you, you will be able perhaps to suggest to them some amelioration of their condition. This may be possible to your ingenious kindness even if their timidity prompts them to delay their aggression, & to attenuate mine, by waiting till they get to Boston. They want to go first to Newport; but I fear its complications for them—& about all ways & means their minds are a touching blank. She is a very exquisite little French Madonna—& he is everything that is admirably sophisticated &

sophisticating. Therefore, dear Mrs. Gardner, look out, *for* him, I mean. I wish I could tell you to look out for yours devotedly

Henry James

LIX

(Ms I S G M, Mamoli Zorzi)

Casa Biondetti.[1]
Venice. June 29*th* [1894]

Dearest Mrs. Gardner.
I tried to write to you yesterday from Asolo—for *auld lang syne*;[2] but the "view" got so between me & my paper that I couldn't get round the purple mountains to dip my pen. I have just been spending three days with Mrs. Bronson—alone with her & Edith[3]—three days of great loveliness. In Venice I have been spending 3 months & I depart in less than a week. It breaks my heart to say it, but therefore I shall not be here when you hold sway at the Barbaro in Sept. & October. I am not even very sure I shall *ever* be here again. Venice, to tell the truth, has been simply blighted,[4] & made a proper little hell (I mean what I say!) by "people"! They have flocked here, these many weeks, in their thousands, & life has been a burden in consequence. The Barbaro is lovelier than ever—but what's the use? I return to England sometime—early—in August—& hide behind a Swiss

mountain till then. Shall you not be in London after I am back? I suppose you are, perversely, just arriving there now. Bien du plaisir! I shall follow you up—in imagination—the rest of the summer! Yours most affectionately

Henry James

NOTES

1 The address, written by hand, refers to the house on the Grand Canal, where James rented a flat and spent three months in June 1894, sorting out the papers, as literary executor, of his friend Constance Fenimore Woolson. Woolson had committed suicide by throwing herself out of a window of Palazzo Semitecolo onto the pavement. James had learnt the news and felt unspeakable horror, and his letters show a sense of possibly unjustified guilt for the death of Woolson, with whom he had shared a house, on different floors, at Bellosguardo, in Florence. The façade on the Grand Canal has a plaque in memory of eighteenth-century painter Rosalba Carriera, who had lived there. See *Letters from the Palazzo Barbaro.*

2 The old song made again popular by Scottish poet Robert Burns.

3 Mrs Bronson's only daughter.

4 This Venetian stay was a real divide in James's perception of the city. From this death, and from other deaths and literary traditions, was generated the Venetian section of *The Wings of the Dove* (1902).

LX

(Ms I S G M)

34 De Vere Gardens. W.[1] *July 14th '94*

I have come home on purpose, dearest lady, to grovel at your feet. Only, to do so, I must know on what tiny spot of this vast expanse they rest.[2] Won't you quickly inform your impatient & devotissimo

Henry James

P.S. I came back night before last—& left Venice just a week before.

NOTES

1 Written by hand. In June 1894 the Gardners arrived in Europe, where they stayed for more than a year, buying nineteen paintings, ten of which were procured by Berenson (Tharp p 177).

2 Instead of going to Austria and Venice, because of Mrs Gardner's sudden ill health, they went to a health spa resort in Germany, at the end of July, and sailed back to the USA on 29th July 1895 (Tharp pp 178, 187).

LXI

(Ms I S G M)

34 de Vere Gardens. W. *Saturday* [1894]

Dear Isabella Gardner.
This is great news, & I rejoice that your arrival is at hand. You apparently are to be here but a moment—but you must get out of that moment many moments for me. Won't you come & take tea with me, & have a quiet talk, at an early stage of the affair? Either on Saturday afternoon, 15*th*, or on Monday ditto, 17*th*, at 5—or 5.30? I mean of course *alone*—with no one bidden to "meet" you—which would spoil all—or at any rate would spoil *you*—& perhaps even me! Do entertain this simple & graceful idea; by which I mean signify to me "I come!" Do, also, have lots to tell me. However, I will take care of that—I will gouge! Remember in particular that you are to be gouged on the subject of Bourget's reception. Your reception will beat it. Yours impatiently

Henry James

LXII

(Ms I S G M)

34, De Vere Gardens. W. *Monday* [1894]

Dear I. G.
On Saturday at *five*—better still. Damn Nickish![1] Yours always

Henry James

NOTE

1 The Hungarian conductor Arthur Nickisch (1855–1922) became famous in Leipzig (1878) and then in Boston in 1889, where he conducted the Boston Symphony Orchestra until 1893, causing controversial comments because of his innovative interpretations. He then directed the Budapest Opera (1893) and those of Leipzig and Berlin from 1895. His *tournées* took him to Moscow and London. He conducted Wagner's operas. He married Amélie Heussner, and had a son, Mitja, who became a pianist. Considering Mrs Gardner's passion for music, it is possible that she had preferred music to a James visit; see Herbert A Kenny, *Boston, Mrs Gardner, Fenway Court and Music* (newworldrecords.org). I would like to thank Angus Wren for suggesting the identification of the name Nickisch, which James spelled incorrectly.

LXIII

(Ms I S G M)

34, De Vere Gardens. W. *Monday* [1894]

Dear Isabella Gardner.
This is a word of thanks for your generous remembrance (in all your rush & crush,) of one so unworthy—a word too of affectionate farewell. I must indeed seem to you shameless not to have *leaped*, before your departure, straight into your spare-room; but everything is really, except for *you*, too complicated & conflicting. You are the great simplifier—I wish you wd. simplify *me*! You literally *have* Bourget a little, I think, but a Minnie also helps that, & I haven't alas, a Minnie. I *couldn't* come while they were there[1]—to perjure myself further—about staying with them; & now that they have gone, you go too. You *oughtn't*—you ought to stay near me. You will never simplify me till you do! But come back—come back. I hold out my hands & I have at any rate still enough of my head, & my heart, above water to be yours most constantly
Henry James

NOTE

1 James promised visits to the Bourgets, and did not keep his promises; see letter 65.

LXIV

(Ms I S G M, Lubbock)

Royal Hospital.
Dublin. *March 23*[d] 1895

Dear Isabella Gardner.
Yes, I have delayed hideously to write to you—since receiving your note of many days ago. But I always delay hideously, & my shamelessness is rapidly becoming (in the matter of letter-writing,) more disgraceful even than my procrastination. I brought your letter with me to Ireland more than a fortnight ago with every intention of answering it on the morrow of my arrival; but I have been leading here a strange & monstrous life of demoralization & frivolity & the fleeting hour has mocked, till today, at my languid effort to stay it, to clutch it, in its passage. I have been paying 3 monstrous visits in a row; & if I needed any further demonstration of the havoc such things make in my life I should find it in this sense of infidelity to a charming friendship of so many years. I return to England to enter a monastery for the rest of my days—& crave your forgiveness

before I take this step. I have been staying in this queer, shabby, sinister, sordid place (I mean Dublin,) with the Lord Lieutenant[1] (poor young Lord Houghton,) for what is called (a fragment, that is, of what is called,) the "Castle Season", & now I am domesticated with very kind & valued old friends, the Wolseleys[2]—Lord W. being Commander of the Forces here (that is head of the little English Army of occupation in Ireland—a 5 years' appointment,) & domiciled in this delightfully quaint & picturesque old structure, of Charles II's time—a kind of Irish Invalides or Chelsea Hospital[3]—a retreat for superannuated veterans, out of which a commodious & stately residence has been carved. We live side by side with the 140 old red-coated, cocked-hatted pensioners—but with a splendid great rococo hall separating us, in which Lady Wolseley gave the other night the most beautiful ball I have ever seen—a fancy-ball in which all the ladies were Sir Joshuas, Gainsboroughs or Romneys[4] & all the men in uniform, court-dress or even[in]g haut-dress. (*I* went as—guess what! alas, nothing smarter than the one black coat in the room.) It is a world of Generals, aide de camps & Colonels, of military colour & sentinel-mounting, which amuses for the moment & makes one reflect afresh that in England those who *have* a good time have it with a vengeance. The episode at the tarnished & ghost-haunted Castle was little to my taste, & was a very queer episode indeed—thanks to the incongruity of a vice-regal "court" (for that's what it considers itself,) utterly boycotted by the Irish (landlord) society—the present viceroy[5] being the nominee of a home-rule government, & reduced to dreary importations from England to fill its gilded halls. There was a ball every night &c; but too much standing on one's hind legs—too much pomp & state, for nothing & nobody. On my return (2 days hence) to my humble fireside I get away again as quickly as possible into the country—to a cot beside a rill, the address of which no man knoweth.[6] There I remain for the next 6 months to come; & nothing of any sort whatever is to happen to me (this is all arranged,) save that you are to come down & stay a day or two with me when you come to England. There *is*, alas, to be no "abroad" for me this year. I rejoice with you in *your* Rome[7]—but my Rome is in the buried past. I spent, however, last June there, & was less excruciated than I feared. Have you seen my old friend Giuseppe Primoli[8]—a great friend in particular of the Bourgets?[9] I daresay you have breakfasted deep with him. May this find you perched on new conquests. It's vain to ask you to write me, or tell me, anything. Let me only ask you therefore to believe me your very affectionate old friend

Henry James

NOTES

1 Lord Houghton, son of James's old friend the poet Richard Monckton Miles (1809–85), also Lord Houghton. Henry James spent over two weeks in Dublin.

2 Garnet Joseph Wolseley (1833–1913), born in Dublin, was Commander of the British army in Ireland from 1890 to 1895, after a long and illustrious career in the army that took him to Burma, the Crimea, and then to India, China, Canada and Africa. In the 1880s he commanded the British forces in Egypt. He published several works, among which are *The Decline and Fall of Napoleon* (1895) and *The Story of a Soldier's Life* (1903). His wife, Lady Louisa (1843–1920), née Erskine, was very active in helping her husband's career; the ball was also meant to "bolster the British presence in Dublin"; see *Dear Munificent Friends* p 239. She was a close friend of James and helped him to furnish Lamb House.

3 The magnificent Chelsea Royal Hospital, in London, founded by Charles II in 1682, as a veterans' home. It was designed by Sir Christopher Wren, and enlarged and modified by Robert Adam between 1765 and 1792.

4 These British painters were extremely popular for their beautiful portraits of ladies, which were copied by women at masked balls. One can think of Edith Wharton's Lily Bart dressing as Mrs Lloyd (by Reynolds) in *The House of Mirth.*

5 Lord Houghton, Lord Lieutenant, also called viceroy, from 1892 to 1895.

6 Perhaps Midhurst, in Sussex, as James wrote to his brother William; see *The Correspondence of William James, Henry and William* II p 358.

7 Mrs Gardner's January–March stay in Rome included a presentation to the Queen of Italy, Margherita, a visit to the Pope and parties at the Roman nobility's palazzi such as the Chigis' (Tharp pp 182–84). Mr Gardner wrote in his diary about meeting Princess Altieri, Marchesi Theodoli and Baron de Schoenberg, at Mrs Elliott's reception on 17th January 1895. Mrs Elliott was the daughter of Julia Ward Howe, who had married the painter John Elliott, and lived in Rome in the Palazzo Rusticucci. (*Travel Diaries 1895* p 3).
8 Mrs Gardner saw Count Primoli in Rome, both at Mrs Elliott's and at his own house for a magic lantern show (ibid pp 3, 9. See also letter 52, note 4).
9 Paul Bourget's novel *Cosmopolis* (1893) is dedicated to Count Primoli.

LXV

(Ms I S G M)

34, De Vere Gardens, W. Feb: 4th *1898*

Dear Isabella Gardner.—
I am touched & charmed by your vivid & generous "tribute". C'est bien le moins that I shld. give you a little pleasure after all the howling benefits & bounties that this many a year your hand has showered on me. And since the wintry ocean *must* so often rage between us, these little amenities do bridge it for an hour & a charming human voice sounds its small silver note—from the western side—in the blast. Well, you shall have something much better than the dreary little Maisie book[1]—though, that, doubtless, has some qualities. I shall do you some much better things than *par le passé*—it is a difficult trick & I'm only, in my declining years, beginning to master it. The winter has hopped from week to week like a bird on a series of twigs—& it's difficult to believe how long it is since I sat in your high saloon at the Savoy & hung on your lips while you hung your Europe[2] before me. As she

hangs before *you* now (incredible woman!—I mean *both* of you) do tell her I languish for her. And I've had a winter without a move. I'm steeped in broken vows & perfidious postponements, & the name of the Bourgets makes me turn quite faint. They've been expecting me at Costebelle[3] since December 20*th*!—But I am, in more ways than one, at my old trick. I promised a note of introduction to you the other day to a very interesting friend of mine, Elizabeth Robins,[4] the actress—mainly of Ibsen—who has just gone to America for 3 or 4 months. She is so interesting & charming, & indeed remarkable, a person & so a head & shoulders above the low level of her vulgar profession that I don't in the least fear she will bore or blight you if she does turn up. Do be kind to her. She's a great (in "littery" circles) social success here. All thanks beforehand & again & always. I wish you had *stayed* this year—London, just now, is quite sympathetic. And Lamb House[5] creeps along! Yours most constantly

Henry James

P.S. The most extraordinary outbreak here of social scandals in the *forging* line—by way of a change: "Bill" Neville (who will get penal servitude) & Lady Sykes & Mrs. Kingscote, daughter of Sir H. Drummond Wolf, who has reproduced Lord Burton's signature to the tune of £ 20,000.[6] Shudder Europa! *Your* bull is not J.B.![7]

NOTES

1 The novel *What Maisie Knew* (1897), about the perception of a little girl whose parents are separated and find new partners. It was published in September 1897 in England and in October 1897 in the USA (Edel-Laurence A49 a and b).

2 The gorgeous *Rape of Europa* by Titian, which Mrs Gardner bought through Bernard Berenson in 1896 (Hadley 1987 p 55–57); Berenson also offered her Titian's *L'amor sacro e l'amor profano*, but Mrs Gardner judged it too expensive for her (ibid pp 183–86).

3 The Bourgets' home on the Côte d'Azur.

4 See letter 49, note 2. *The New York Times* (31st March 1898) appreciated only partially Miss Robins's acting in *Hedda Gabler*: "Miss Robins's interpretation … is as clear and as comprehensible as need be; the meaning of every one of Hedda's moods is graphically expressed, but the representation lacks breadth, eloquence and sustained force in the most difficult passages … Otherwise Miss Robins's acting is remarkably good. It is very elaborate in pose, gesture, and tone, without ever seeming stiff or artificial; and it is worthy of cordial praise" (p 6).

5 James's house at Rye, in Sussex, which he rented in 1898 and then bought in 1899.

6 James refers to two famous cases of bankruptcy, the reports of which appeared in *The New York Times*. Lady Sykes (c 1856–1912), née Christina Cavendish-Bentick, married Sir Tatton Sykes (1826–1913), thirty years older than she was, 'a man of eccentric character', as mentioned in *The Times* of 13th January 1898, during their trial. Lady Sykes had allegedly forged her

husband's signature on a loan of £79,350, as reported in *The New York Times* of 12th January 1898. Apparently she also tried to sell the family jewels to pay off her debts, as *The Times* reported on 12th February 1898.

In 1898 an eighteen-year-old solicitor's clerk served writs on Adeline Georgiana Isabella Kingscote (1860–1908), daughter of Sir Henry Drummond Charles Wolff (1830–1908), at Bury Knowle House, where she had lived since 1895, after being with her husband, Colonel Howard Kingscote, in India. Mrs Kingscote, notorious for her charm and extravagance, had borrowed money from several men, finally going bankrupt in 1899, and selling all the contents of Bury Knowle. During her Indian residence Mrs Kingscote collected and published *Folklore of Southern India* (1890) with Pandit Natesa Sastri; she gave birth to a son in Bangalore, and published *The English Baby in India and How to Rear It* (1893). She later published several novels under pseudonyms.

The other person and initials in James's postscript have not been identified.

7 The *bull* in Titian's *Europa*, and perhaps a pun on the use of 'bull' in the stock market, to indicate one who "endeavours by speculative purchases or otherwise, to raise the price of stocks" (*Oxford English Dictionary*).

LXVI

(Ms I S G M)

34, De Vere Gardens, W. Feb:10th 1898

Dear Mrs. Gardner.

I have written you so fully about Miss Robins that this is a mere quick gesture to place her hand in yours. When once it *is* so placed the next will come of itself. More than ever then shall I value each of you—for helping me to do such a kindness to the other. *Do* let Miss Robins take for me an impression of the Titian. I *have* a lovely one—yours—but I want as many as there are photographs for a kinetoscope.[1] That's already the number—of impressions—I have of *you*. Give *time*—& take it—& feel that all of it is both for & from—Yours more than ever

Henry James

NOTE

1 Large photographs of paintings and buildings were popular in this period, as Mrs Gardner's travel albums show. The kinetoscope was based on a peep show of photographs, producing the illusion of movement. The first show was in 1893 in Brooklyn. In 1903 and then in 1912 the kinetoscope of the Delhi Durbar was shown in London: Mrs Curtis went to see the latter in London, because her grandson Henry Osborne was in the pageant—" … she will have to go *daily* in order not to miss him … as he shimmers beautifully past"; *Letters to Miss Allen* p 118. James was interested in photography and perhaps the early cinema; see his correspondence with Alvin Coburn for the images of the New York Edition of his works; see Edel *Letters IV* pp 426–428.

LXVII

(Ts I S G M)

34, de Vere Gardens, W. April 3, 1898

Dear and wonderful lady.
You amiably appeal to me to "write"—and behold what my writing consists of. It consists of this, and of this only, nowadays—and if you will take it in this form, you get more, as it were, for the money. But please believe I wouldn't so outrage you were it not either Remington[1] or silence. Silence indeed—my own too ungracious—has been hugely on my mind, that is on my conscience, ever since the hyacinthine Lapsley[2] mentioned to me some little time since your lamentable little accident,[3] which was to be justified, I think, only on the ground of your being by necessity always up to something, and of *its* being the only thing one could think of that had not yet happened to you. Besides, since you told me about the Europa,[4] everything somehow works round to that. My imagination shoved roseleaves, as it were, under the spine of a lady for whom lying fractured was but an occasion the more to foregather with Titian.

Seriously I hope you weren't very bad—that it was nothing more than the Europa could bandage up with a piece of that purple of which you gave me so memorable an account. You have moreover so many compensations for all the miseries that *don't* overtake you, that I ask myself on what scale you must be organising them now for the one that did. Is the Pope going to sell you one of the rooms of the Vatican? Do seek your compensation—when it's time—on this side of the world, where the commodity appears, on the whole, to be most dealt in. I write you in these flippant accents, but at the moment I do so, and perhaps still more at the moment you receive them, who knows how much we may not both be under the shadow of the black Spanish business.[5] It's all a great horror—one can only feel, isn't it so?—save in so far as mitigated by the sense that we have, this time, nationally, behaved remarkably well, and with more procrastination—especially after the Maine business—than I think any other of the big guns would have shown. I was an hour or two yesterday with John Hay,[6] but didn't squeeze out of him much of the weakminded comfort that I desired. But ne parlons pas de ça; it isn't at all remedial for you; and there may be only too much to say about it later. I rejoice you didn't wholly fail of a glimpse of Miss Robins—especially as you appear to have appreciated her—but I'm sorry your glimpse was only single and slight. She is quite the most interesting and distinguished "nature" I have ever known connected with her unnatural trade. And I know nothing of what she is doing là-bas beyond a dim apprehension of dusky Ibsenite rites. I shall hear when she comes back, and it will be a lively tale; only I'm afraid, meanwhile, that the baleful breath of Cuba will blow out Hedda Gabler. Still, I console myself—that is try to correct myself—with a queer sort of a recollection of how of old, during the war in periods of excitement, victory or defeat, the theatres used to be crowded as a kind of refuge from reality. A propos of them, but two nights since, I had a small swarry in the form of Mrs. Clifford[7] and her two daughters to dinner and lovely Lapsley down from Cambridge (where he is spending a month) to meet them and be taken with them to a big bad farce of Pinero's.[8] It was extremely nice of him to come so far for so little (he amiably spent the night with me)—but of course everything in him, and of him *is* extremely nice. He is a particularly pleasant being, for whose acquaintance I thank you; and I'm only sorry that he bids fair soon to vanish into the horrible American space. He is so charmingly civilized that I somehow don't fit him into the small provincial, professional niche that he so modestly speaks of as the best thing he can for a long time expect. I have had a winter, personally, without a fracture—but on the other hand absolutely without a movement, which perhaps explains it, or is an alternative equally bad.

It has been the quietest that, in all my London years, I have ever lived through—for which I have quite passionately loved it.[9] I stand, in consequence, quite lost and perjured with the proud pair at Costebelle.[10] It's the third year I was to have gone to see them and proved false and feeble. It has been impossible—but that doesn't make it any better; and meanwhile I feel cut off from them by abysses of silence and darkness—for I don't believe they will come to England again this summer. I'm very sorry to have no news of them to give you. But I have little of any news. Nothing, thank heaven, happens to me. I'm most ungracefully busy—writing a good deal. You shall have it all—since you can work some of it in, as soon as it has *book*-form. It has to have other tiresome forms first, which I pray God remain invisible to you. This is "picture Sunday", and I go in an hour or two, though I loathe the general practice, to Sargent's studio, taking with me a little paintress-cousin[11] who is working hard in Paris and showing high promise. Sargent will have this year a show of extraordinary fine portraits of men—one of them, Wertheimer,[12] the Bond Street Jew dealer, being in particular, I think, one of the most masterly things of "this or any age." He has done Miss Leiter,[13] Mrs. Curzon's sister, in a very brilliant kind of Gainsborough way. But there is also a slight Watteau element in the thing against which the six feet of stature and the little intensely modern Fifth Avenue face of the young woman rather militates. Yesterday was likewise picture-Saturday, and I was at Alfred Parsons'[14] (who will cover himself, thank heaven, this year, with glory) where I found the brave and universally adventurous Millet,[15] up in town to bring out not only pictures, but deadly realities in the way of desperate daughters—that is of *one*, who, however, looms to me as rather a regiment. Still, people live through these things. I am in town a month or two more—then I crawl under the little tent that, as I think I told you in October, I have found a quiet corner to pitch. Goodbye, daughter of Titian. I hope, by the way, the picture is not going to Madrid. Make me some sign or other, however small—even a carrier pigeon—through the din of battle, and believe me always affectionately yours

Henry James

NOTES

1 This letter was typed on a Remington. While writing *What Maisie Knew* in 1896, James got writer's cramp; as he wrote: the Remington "crept into my existence though the crevice of a lame hand" (Edel *Letters IV* p 45). The first amanuensis was the Scottish MacAlpine.

2 Gaillard Thomas Lapsley (1871–1949), a young friend of James's introduced by Mrs Gardner, was a medieval history scholar, who had gone to Harvard and taught in California until 1904, when he became a fellow and tutor at Trinity College, Cambridge. He published *The Country Palatine of Durham* (1900) and essays and articles, some of which were published in *Crown, Community and Parliament in the Late Middle Ages.* MacAlpine spelt 'hyacinthine' without the 'h' after the 't'. As for its meaning, it can indicate a blond colour or, as Howard Sturgis used it in *Belchamber* (1904), a 'white' or 'hoary' colour.

3 On 7th February 1898, Mrs Gardner broke "the fibula of one of her legs just above the ankle"; she did not give up her normal life and went to hear Wagner in a wheelchair (Tharp pp 204–05).

4 See letter 65.

5 James is referring to the Cuban war, which began with the explosion of the warship *USS Maine*, on 15th February 1898, in the port of Havana, Cuba. The ship represented the US support of the revolution against Spain. The press claimed it was a sabotage action by the Spanish, although it was never clear who caused the explosion. The war of the USA against Spain started in April and ended in August, with the Treaty of Paris (December 1898), and it marked the growing expansionism of the US. Spain ceded Cuba, and Puerto Rico, Guam and the Philippines.

6 See letter 23, note 6.

7 Lucy Lane Clifford (1846–1929), an old London friend of James's. After the death of her husband, a professor of mathematics and a philosopher, in 1879, she earned a living for herself and her children by writing novels, such as *Mrs Keith's Crime* (1885) and *Aunt Anne* (1893). 'Swarry' was used ironically for the French *soirée* (*OED*).

8 Arthur Wing Pinero (1855–1934), British playwright well known for his plays and farces, among which are *Trelawney of the Wells* (1898) and *The Gay Lord Quex* (1899).

9 In the autumn of 1897 James had dictated to MacAlpine *The Turn of the Screw*, which was published in *Collier's Weekly* January–April 1898. In the spring he was working on *The Awkward Age*.

10 See letter 65, note 3.

11 Ellen Emmet, painter, called 'Bay', daughter of Ellen James Temple (1850–1920), who was the younger sister of James's cousin Minnie Temple.

12 The portrait of Asher Wertheimer (1898, oil on canvas, Tate Gallery, London) was exhibited at the Royal Academy and immediately judged a masterpiece. Wertheimer was a famous Bond Street antiques dealer, who commissioned from Sargent portraits of his wife and ten members of his family; see Ormond-Kilmurray 2002 pp 132–34, Kilmurray-Ormond n 54 pp 148–49; Ormond-Kilmurray 2003 pp 53–55, 90, 125, 136, 139, 142–44, 202–04, 208.

13 The beautiful oil portrait (1898) of Daisy Leiter (1867–1968), then Countess of Suffolk and Berkshire, daughter of a rich Chicagoan Levi Z Leiter. She met her husband in India, at her sister Mary's. Mary had married George Nathaniel Curzon,

viceroy of India (1898–1905); see Ormond-Kilmurray 2002 pp 231–32, 272.

14 Alfred Parsons (1847–1920), British landscape painter and illustrator, part of the 'Broadway colony' of 1885–86, in the picturesque village of Broadway in the Cotswolds, where Sargent painted *Carnation, Lily, Lily, Rose*, and where James also visited. In *Our Artists in Europe*, published in *Harper's New Monthly Magazine 79* June 1889, James wrote about the village and Parsons: "A very old English village, lying among its meadows and hedges, in the very heart of the country, is responsible directly and indirectly for some of the most beautiful work in black and white with which I may concern myself here; that is for much of the work of Mr Abbey and Mr Frank Parsons" (p 50).

15 Frank (Francis) Millet (1846–1912), American painter and illustrator, friend of Sargent who made a portrait of his wife and son (Ormond-Kilmurray *The Early Portraits* pp 170–71, and Ormond-Kilmurray 2002 p 60), and of John Abbey, whose Farnham House and then Russell House were the welcoming centres of the Broadway colony of artists. Millet, an adventurous man, was a drummer boy during the American Civil War, and a war correspondent during the Russian-Turkish war of 1877–78. He studied at Harvard and the Antwerp Academy, where he studied art, and was director of the decorations at the Chicago Exposition of 1893. He married Elizabeth Merrill in Paris in 1879 (Saint-Gaudens and Mark Twain being his witnesses) and had three sons and one daughter, Kate. He died in the Titanic.

LXVIII

(Ms I S G M)

Lamb House, Rye.[1] Feb 2^{d} 1899.

My dear Isabella Gardner—

I was lately in London—from which I have been for months & months wholly absent & detached—& there, long after the event, I heard for the first time of the disaster that has lately overtaken you.[2] It is only now, at last, that I write, & the fact was made known to me a fortnight ago—with the shock—I mean the added shock—of my ignorance & silence. I can't tell you why I didn't *instantly* write you—though I can partly tell you—it was because I felt that I must *already* have seemed to you dumb & distant, & that consciousness weighed upon me & paralysed me. And now I have nothing but horror for my delay. I beg you to believe that all the while it has made you only *more* present to me—& made *him* so, by the same strange force. Very, very charmingly present to me is he as I talk of the kindness & courtesy that, like the generous gentleman he was, (& all abundance & health & gaiety as I last saw him) he for such long, long years always showed me. I haven't a memory of him that isn't delightful & mixed with delightful things. I always saw him in beautiful, happy, beneficent conditions & places—& he remains one of my images (none too numerous) of those moving in great affairs with a temper that matched them & yet never lost its consideration for *small* affairs & for the people condemned to them. What a change in your life!—that is all I dare say to you. Please, however, let me add that I think of you with every tenderness of friendship—& with innumerable visions & memories of all past brightnesses & pleasantnesses of which he was a part. I greatly want to see you—& I hope with all my heart that Europe will at no very distant day draw you again. I am wholly out of London just now—& next week I go to Italy for 2 or 3 months. This little old house[3] & this quiet work have proved a perfect fit for me, & I hate to leave them, even for Venice & Rome. But that will pass (I mean *at* Venice & Rome) & I shall come back for a deep relapse. Would I could receive you here! Well, I hold fast to the belief that I shall yet, & I am, dear Isabella Gardner, more than ever your affectionate old friend

Henry James

NOTES

1 All the letters from Lamb House are written on Lamb House letterhead paper.

2 James learnt about Mr Gardner's sudden death from apoplexy on 10th December 1898.

3 As mentioned (letter 65, note 5), James had bought Lamb House in 1899.

LXIX

(Ms I S G M)

Lamb House, Rye. March 6th *1899.*

My dear Isabella Gardner—

It has been a great balm to get your letter & feel again in communication & contact with you. I sit here late tonight scribbling you this word of thanks for it—before I go tomorrow, to Folkestone (but an hour distant) to cross, on the day following, to Paris—to Venice & Rome. I sat here 10 days & 10 nights ago writing letters (with the same departure fixed,) only to discover at two o' clock in the a.m. that the house was on fire.[1] It has taken all the time since then to weep over the ruins (only of two rooms,) & arrange for reconstruction. Pray with me that I make no similar discovery tonight. Old houses have strange—in walls & floors—tricks and traps. But it's now *1* a.m., & all's well. I mainly want to tell you how I rejoice that you see, at all, a time for coming out. May it come round with a steady roll. I spend but a week in Paris & then go (for 4 or 5 days,) to Costebelle.[2] The odious Dreyfus[3] affair is rather in the air between me & that retreat—I don't feel about it as I gather our friends there do. But it is everywhere—in that queerer & queerer country—& one must duck one's head & pass quickly. I go thence to *Asolo*[4]—so you see I've work cut out! I stay *là-bas* till June, & shall have plenty to tell you when we meet. You *must* see this blessed hermitage. I figure you in abysses of affairs.[5] Well, you'll be good for them, & they can't hurt *you*. But don't be their slave, & arrange things so that you can, on this side of the world, stay longer than you used. Good-night—I must lock my portmanteaux. Yours, dear Mrs. Gardner, always & ever

Henry James

NOTES

1 At 2.30 in the morning, while James was still awake, there was a dangerous fire under the floor. He had to postpone his departure, as he also wrote to the Curtises from Paris on 16th March 1899 (*Letters from the Palazzo Barbaro* pp 155–156).

2 To the Bourgets, see letter 65, note 3.

3 1899 was the apex of the 'affaire Dreyfus', when the trial was resumed against Alfred Dreyfus (1859–1935), a French officer from a Jewish family who had been charged with high treason and condemned to deportation. The trial was reopened thanks to the famous *J'accuse* (1898) by Emile Zola, and pardon was granted, but Dreyfus's military rank was reinstated only in 1906. This very well-known case divided public opinion. Bourget was against the defenders of Dreyfus, who were considered enemies of religion and the established order. James did go to Costebelle in April 1899.

4 To Mrs Bronson's, at 'La Mura', see letter 27, note 3.

5 After the death of her husband, Mrs Gardner bought the land on which Fenway Court was to be built; the purchase commenced on 31st January 1899, and was concluded on 26th February 1900 (Tharp p 339).

LXX

(Ms I S G M)

Lamb House, Rye. *July 10th* [1899]

My dear Isabella Gardner.
I returned 2 days ago from 4 months in Italy & your letter of the 25th June was the most eminent feature of the table-full of postal-matter awaiting me here. Welcome, welcome, fifty times welcome back to this warm side of the globe.[1] Please believe that I hold out my hands to you most affectionately. I am *here*, of course—London is anything but appetizing to me now with this so much better alternative, and 34 De Vere Gardens is let (these 6 months)[2] to the end of the month, so that I am without a London gîte even if I were in need of one. What I greatly hope is—it would give me infinite joy—that you would see your way to coming down here either for a night or for a day. I can put you up very decently, & can even manage a maid if she isn't very haughty—but if you shld. prefer *not* to sleep the thing *has* been feasible, in these long summer days, by several fair & patient pilgrims. Mrs. Mason, Mrs. Fields & Miss Jewett,[3] & nameless, numberless others, achieved

it last summer. There is an excellent train from Charing X at *11* a.m., which brings you to my very door in time for luncheon at 1.30.; & there are two that—including one via *Hastings*—take you comfortably back in time for a lateish dinner—if you're not dining out. By the 11 out you change at Ashford. It is a good deal of train for so few hours of converse perhaps—but, in fine, they *have* done it—they *do* do it. It would be better, of course, to sleep, & I should be delighted to help you thereto—so think of it well. On the 17*th* comes (by the 11 a.m.) our young friend Lapsley.[4] Couldn't you come *with* him? Perhaps, however, that's a day too late for you. Couldn't you therefore come *Saturday—?* Do, *do*, *do.* Won't you give my very kind regards to the George Gardners[5] & tell them how I should rejoice if they will come *with* you. I can chair & table & feed & sofa you all—& this little nook is quaint and charming. If not Saturday, Friday?—only you *must* come. The Curtises did!—Apropos of whom, what cross purposes we are at, you and I—I who spent almost the whole month of April at the Barbaro's! But you have come abroad this time I devoutly hope, for a long straight stay. Perhaps if you *can* come Saturday our dear delightful Lapsley will be able to come too. However, act as wholly suits your own convenience. Sunday trains, I am sorry to say, are no use. May this promptly meet you at Southampton & convey you the tenderest greeting of yours, dear Isabella Gardner, very constantly

Henry James

NOTES

1 Mrs Gardner went to Europe with Lena Little (1865–1920), a contralto singer; spent August at the Barbaro in Venice; went to Paris, Brussels and England, with a short stay at Bournemouth in December; and was back home on 18th December 1899 (Tharp p 223).

2 The place was indeed let for a whole year to the Stopford Brooks; see *Dearly Beloved Friends* p 28.

3 See letter 32 for Mrs Mason. The Bostonian Annie Fields (1834–1915), née Adams, was the widow of James Thomas Fields, editor of the *Atlantic Monthly* and publisher (see letter 100); Sarah Orne Jewett (1849–1909) was the American author of *The Country of the Pointed Firs* (1896) and other works, and friend and lover of Annie Fields, after the death of Mr Fields in 1881. Fields and Jewett had gone to Rye in September 1898. In 1910 Mrs Fields wrote in her diary about James's visit to her in Boston: "I have seldom enjoyed an hour more than the one spent in the light of his fine sympathy. He asked about Sarah's letters—said he should like to see them—that he wished to write a few words of introduction or what I might call an 'éclaircissement' of her gift", quoted in Roman p 160. Her portrait was painted by Sargent in 1890; see Ormond-Kilmurray 2002 pp 45–46.

4 See letter 67.

5 John Gardner's older brother, George Augustus Gardner, with his wife Eliza Endicott Peabody.

LXXI

(Ms I S G M)

Lamb House, Rye. *Friday* [1899]

Dearest Mrs. Gardner.
This is brave news! The thing is perfectly possible—my brother & his wife did it a month ago, arriving, that is, from *Paris.* I don't know what time your Ostend boat[1] is due—but there are *2* hitherward trains after 5 o'clock (from *Ashford Junction*, 15 minutes from Folkestone, to which the Folkestone train will bring you & where you change for Rye (having *then* just 30 minutes run to *me.*) So you see it's distinctly near; & I rejoice unspeakably at your happy inspiration & my own still happier opportunity. *But*, on the other hand, the 25*th* is a *Saturday* &, on spending the night here, you *can't* get on, on the Sunday (*at all*) to town. This is a pious Xtian land—so much the better for *me.* There are absolutely *no* Sunday trains to town; you will spend therefore the Sunday here, & go up very comfortably by the 9.38 on Monday a.m. So is it written in your book of fate. A day here won't kill you at all—& I can *perfectly* put up

your maid along-side of you. Voilà. Bon voyage. Only very kindly *wire* me from Folkestone on arriving—there are lots of little telegraph boys about. Then I shall know by about what train to meet you at my little station—which, however, is only 5 minutes from my house—so I can go to each. It *will* be a windfall to see you! Always yours

Henry James

NOTE

1 Mrs Gardner arrived via Dover. On 28th November 1899, James wrote to Charles Eliot Norton that he was going to meet Mrs Gardner, "who arrives from Brussels, charged with the spoils of the Flemish school" (Edel *Letters IV* p 124). See Introduction.

LXXII

(Ms I S G M)

Lamb House, Rye. *Monday* [1899]

Dear Isabella Gardner.

The 28th or 29th will do *better* even than the 25th: & if you must go up to town hence the very next morning, why, you can do so on one of those week-days better than on the Sabbatical 26th. They are a Tuesday & a Wednesday—only let me know a day before *which*—& retain my letter of 2 days ago (in answer to your first) for such mild instruction as it contains. I hope this will catch you before your departure from Brussels. How mysterious & complicated you are! You need, really, a few hours contact with my rustic simplicity. I long greatly for your Bourget news. If my "instructions" are not sufficient do you want any further? *Only specify your day & wire from Folkestone—on arrival.* Yours impatiently

Henry James

LXXIII

(Ms I S G M)

Lamb House, Rye. Nov. 23^{d} *1899.*

Dear un-almanacked lady!
Better & better! No; the 26th being a Sunday, the 29th is *not* another! We have a good many in this country, but not quite every 3^{d} day. Come then, by all means, on the 29th from Dover—but very kindly do as I originally asked—let me be sure that *is* your day & kindly *wire* me on your arrival at Folkestone. I can put you up to perfection & shall be enchanted at the sight & sound of you. I rejoice you are to be with the Ralphs[1] & I send them mille tendresses—all three. Believe me yours always & always

Henry James

P.S. The 29th is a Wednesday, & the 30th a Thursday!

NOTE

1 Ralph Curtis (1854–1922), painter, son of Ariana and Daniel Sargent Curtis, the owners of the Palazzo Barbaro, and his wife, Lisa Colt Rotch (1871–1933), whose portraits were painted by Ralph and his friend Sargent. In 1898 Sargent painted the beautiful *An Interior in Venice*, which portrayed Ariana and Daniel, and their son and daughter-in-law, in the magnificent salon of the Palazzo Barbaro. See Kilmurray-Ormond pp 151–52. James loved the painting; see Mamoli Zorzi in *Sargent's Venice* p 142.

LXXIV

(Ts I S G M, Edel, Carter)

Lamb House, Rye. November 27th, 1899.

Dear wild and wandering friend,

Here again is an intensely legible[1] statement of your needful proceeding at Dover on the arrival, at the nominal 2.30, of your boat from Calais. It will consist simply of your looking out for me, as hard as possible,—if not as soft!—from the deck of the vessel. I shall be on the dock to meet you, penetrating with eagle eye the densest crowd: so that, after all, *your* looks won't so much matter. I shall try to have mine of my best. I shall await you, in other words,—reach out the friendliest of hands to you as you step, de votre pied léger, from the plank. The rest is silence. You will have nothing whatever more to do but what I mildly but firmly bid you. If you only mind what I tell you, all will still be well. We shall combine convenient promptitude with convenient deliberation and reach Rye in time for tea and tartines. Be therefore at peace—and keep your powder dry. I wish you as smooth and swift and simple a business of it, all through, as may be possible to so complex an organism. The weather here is lovely now and the Channel a summer sea—which I trust we shall still profit by. *Thursday* then, I repeat, on the Dover Pier at 2.30. Yours more than ever impatiently[2]

Henry James

NOTES

1 Dictated typecript.

2 Mrs Gardner stayed at Lamb House for a couple of days, as James wrote to Hendrik Andersen on 22nd December 1899; see *Beloved Boy* p 9.

LXXV

(MS I S G M)

Lamb House, Rye. December 27th *1899*

Dear Isabella Gardner.
I ought indeed, before this, to have written to you; & never meant, in the world, to have let you leave England without any further sign from me. But you simply announced your flight to "Bournemouth"—without an address there, & I knew not how to follow you rightly, & was overdone, in London, during the remaining few days before your embarkation, with complications, cares & labours—to say nothing of fog & gloom & depression & rheumatism. By the time I was free you had gone, & I had, with infinite relief, returned hither. Here I remain for the present—at any rate through January. If I find I funk for February & March, such a continuity of *vie de province*,[1] I shall go up & perch in town, where light may, by that time, have broken. The concentrated gloom of Xmas is beginning to trail its black mantle a little from off us: I've only got through it by remembering that the kind cheer of

your presence settled here, a little before, long enough to scatter a benediction—& that the same benignant influence may some day be renewed. I coax it along—the after-sense of it, still; & try to keep up your echo.—I hope with all my heart that your homeward journey was not inconvenient beyond measure & that your own pictured halls[2] now again possess, undisturbed, their mistress. May every fog-demon have completely ceased to breathe on you, & may the coming time lay nothing but soft carpets & green lawns for your feet—with a patch or two of old mossy marble thrown in. I think of you as a figure on a wondrous *cinque-cento* tapestry[3]—& of myself as one of the small quaint accessory domestic animals, a harmless worm or mild little rabbit in the corner. Well, dearest lady, the worm, or the rabbit is very proud & happy to be in the same general composition with you; & is always & always affectionately yours

Henry James

NOTES

1 Surely a conscious allusion to Balzac's series *Scènes de la vie de province* (1834–37).

2 By this date Mrs Gardner had collected most of her treasures, with the help of Bernard Berenson, and also of Ralph Curtis, Richard Norton and Joseph Lindon Smith, and had engaged architect Willard Sears to draw up the plans for her Fenway Court Museum.

3 James was perhaps thinking of the little animals represented in the famous *cinquecento* tapestries of *La dame à la licorne*, which the Musée de Cluny, Paris, bought in 1882.

LXXVI

(Ms I S G M)

Lamb House, Rye, Sussex. July 23^{d} *1904.*[1]

Dearest Isabella Gardner!

I am more touched than I can say by the sweetness of your letter, & made miserably conscious of my long failure to make you the sign of faithful remembrance, in fact of constant yearning of the spirit, that I have so dreadfully long owed you. All your recent splendid history[2] & accomplished glory have filled me with the impulse to show you how admiringly, here in my far-off hermitage, I think of you, & how I have devoured every echo of your greatness that has penetrated my solitude. Many, thank heaven, have done so—so that I have, inwardly, quite lived with you and fed on you; & I think that the reason I have remained, none the less, so dumb is simply that I scarce knew what to say that would be in proportion & *on the scale.* I have been really ashamed to toss you, across the footlights, a 50-cent bouquet, & the proper mountain of flowers & expensive serenade under your windows, seemed, alas, more than I was able to manage. And now you come & make the 50-cent bouquet easy to me; you reach over & take it in your hand, & I let it go for what it is worth—with tears in my eyes for the grace of your proceeding. It is an immense pleasure to me to be able, in the light of this happy incident, to believe that I *shall* really see you again at no very distant day. For I do truly suppose myself to be embarking for New York on August 25*th* (or rather 24*th*)[3]—having gone so far as to take my passage. I fear really to believe these things till they actually take place, but I am tenderly nursing my project, at all events, & there is now only a month for it to turn & rear & betray me in, & that isn't very much time. It isn't more than time for me positively to go. I am booked to spend *September* from the 1*st* hour with my brother William at Chocorua N.H.,[4] but I shall come back from here the 1*st* days of October & then will come & see you with, I needn't tell you what joy. Be well & happy & mighty till then & continue to keep a place in your generosity for your ever-affectionate old friend

Henry James

NOTES

1 By mid-July James had finished his novel *The Golden Bowl* (Horne p 401) and was planning to go to the USA.

2 Mrs Gardner had built Fenway Court between 1900 and 1902, spending her first night there on 18th November 1901, and opening the museum on 1st January 1903.

3 James sailed on 24th August, from Southampton, on the *Kaiser Wilhelm II*, arriving at Hoboken, New Jersey, on 30th August. This trip was partly arranged by W D Howells for lectures in different places. From this renewed experience of his own country, which James had not seen for over twenty years, was born the wonderful book *The American Scene* (1907).

4 James's brother William had a family summer home in the White Mountains of New Hampshire. On 5th July 1897, William wrote to Henry from Chocorua: "the air is sweet and the aromatic asperity of everything most beautiful" (*The Correspondence of William James, William and Henry* III p 11). Henry loved the place, in spite of finding it sometimes "sad and lonely" (3rd July 1902 ibid p 207).

LXXVII

(Ms I S G M)

Chocorua, N.H.[1] *Sept: 16: 1904*

Dear Isabella Gardner—
You wrote me, beautifully, before I left England, & I certainly answered you, as beautifully as I could. And now the strange thing has come true, & I *am* here, & I have been here, (in the U.S.,) 18 days—& 16 of them specially *here*—delightfully. But I depart to-day & get nearer to you. How am I to do it?—& when *may* I, if you are still so magnanimously minded, come & see you at home? I go to Jackson N.H., to Cotuit, Mass, & to Salisbury, Conn.,[2] on leaving this—each for 3 days or so; but from the very 1st days of October I shall be within hail—& always accessible by a word to my brother's house—*95 Irving St. Cambridge, Mass.* Possibly you may have quitted Brookline by that time, but wherever you may be I wish you fortitude & peace & am ever so constantly yours

Henry James

NOTES

1 The printed letterhead—Lamb House, Rye, Sussex—is deleted.

2 James went to Jackson, New Hampshire, to Cotuit, Massachusetts, and to Salisbury, Connecticut, where he paid a visit to his Emmet relatives in Salisbury (see following letter). He went to Jackson to see Katherine Wormeley Prescott, Ariana Curtis's sister, and a novelist and translator, and to Cotuit, on Cape Cod, where Howard Sturgis was staying with his half-sister, Lucy Lyman Paine, who was married to Charles R Codman; see Powers 1990 p 39 and Horne p 405.

LXXVIII

(Ms I S G M)

95 Irving St.[1]
Cambridge Sept. 30*th* [1904] *p.m.*

Dear Isabella Gardner.

I haven't been a Brute since the arrival of your so beautiful & gentle letter: I've only been a Victim—a victim of many things, people & discharged avalanches of postal matter, & in particular of a deluge of *Proofs*[2] of a forthcoming long & pressingly hurried Book, which I have had utterly to give myself to these last 6 days (each day since I returned from Chocorua,) & which have kept me occupied from 9 a.m. to 6 p.m., & left me then too spent & tired to touch a pen that evening. Hence now a pile of unacknowledged letters. But yours comes first—my corvée ended this afternoon. The Deuce has it that I go tomorrow—by dreadfully deferred engagement, to stay with some relations in Connecticut[3]—to stay that is for 3 or 4 days. I then come back here, & then go to spend *one* day with my younger brother[4] at Concord. It would *enchant* me to come throw myself on your hospitality immediately after *that*, if that is still convenient to you, as the noble liberality of your letter seems to indicate. I am afraid it isn't safe for me to count on being clear before tomorrow *week*, Saturday October 8th, but if I hear nothing from you to the contrary I will present myself at your door late in the afternoon of that day, & will abide with you, if you tolerate me, till Friday the 14th a.m. following—being committed to go [to] Lenox[5] for some days on the 15th (which matches admirably your visit to New York.) I yearn to be in your presence again & feel, in all my bones, that the hundred things (I devoutly hope) you will tell me are to be the most interesting I have ever listened to. Don't write another note unless you *can't* have me. Trust me to turn up if you *are* accessible by the sign of silence—& believe me yours always & ever

Henry James

NOTES

1 Written by hand.

2 The proofs of *The Golden Bowl.*

3 See letter 77, note 2.

4 Robertson (1846–1910), who had problems with alcohol and mental health throughout his life.

5 Lenox, in the Berkshires, where James's novelist friend Edith Wharton had her house, 'The Mount'. James went there with Howard Sturgis (Lewis p 140). Although Wharton was invited to the gala opening of Fenway Court, there was not much sympathy between her and Mrs Gardner (ibid p 115).

LXXIX

(Ms I S G M)

95 Irving Street[1]--
Cambridge [1904]

Dear Isabella Gardner—
’Tis well, ’tis most excellently & admirably well, & this Saturday & Sunday, to which I just return under this roof, will prove a godsend to me for appalling arrears of unanswered letters. I am sorry you had so much as another note to write, & am yours—in the definite intention of turning up day after tomorrow Monday afternoon lateish,—yours very constantly

Henry James

Saturday a.m.

NOTE

1 Written by hand.

LXXX

(Ms I S G M)

Cambridge[1] [1904]
Monday.

Dear Isabella Gardner.
Don't *mind*, please, at all, my overcoat (light brown mackintosh-thing,) I left in so unmannerly a fashion in your hall—Howard Sturgis[2] told me you were so very kindly troubled about it. I have but just 3 days ago returned here from a longish stay at Lenox,[3] & am hoping, trying hard, to spend as much as possible of this month, & even a little of next, here. So I will make the first possible occasion for a pilgrimage over to Green Hill, & will then possess myself of my garment & relieve you of the care of it. I am funking Biltmore[4] awfully & trying to back out of the too long journey & sacrifice of *present* precious time. Cling to me, you, & help to save me. I hope all things are well with you—but when are they ever not? The thought of this is a joy to yours always

Henry James

NOTES

1 Written by hand diagonally at the top of the letter.

2 Howard Overing Sturgis (1855–1920), a writer and a dear friend of James. Sturgis asked James's advice regarding his novels and stories, in particular *Belchamber* (1904). James never spared his criticism, even to his closest friends, or men he might have been in love with, such as Sturgis and Andersen; see the correspondence in *Dearly Beloved Friends* pp 115–74, and *Beloved Boy.*

3 James stayed with Mrs Wharton at Lenox in October for more than ten days, also enjoying the magnificent, gold-like 'foliage', which had inspired one of Hawthorne's tales on King Midas.

4 Biltmore, the luxurious mansion of George Washington Vanderbilt (1862–1914), son of the railway tycoon, built by Richard Morris Hunt, from 1889 to 1895, in the mountains near Asheville, North Carolina. James went there in February 1905, and wrote an appalled letter to his brother William about the building ("what can be the application of a French chateau to life in this irretrievably niggery wilderness"; Edel *Letters IV* p 344) and about the climate. He modified his judgement on the "tortures" of Biltmore in *American Scene.*

LXXXI

(Ms I S G M)

Monday a.m.

Dear Mrs. Gardner—
You are most kind. I should be delighted to go to the Country Club—but I am afraid that—as you intend it—an engagement to dine (at Mrs. J. W. Howe's)[1] at 6.30 will be an obstacle. I have an idea that you mean to dine there—i.e. at the C.C. If you *don't*, I will go with pleasure at your side. I am going out at 4.30 & will stop at that moment chez vous. You can then take me or not, according as your plan may have been. Tout à vous, Madam

H. James

NOTE

1 Julia Ward Howe, see letter 11, note 4.

LXXXII

(Ms I S G M)

21, East Eleven Street — Telephone, 2750 Gramercy.

May 15th[1] [1905]

Dear Isabella G.

It was impossible, alas, it was impossible—I will tell you how utterly so when we meet. I arrived in Boston for a day or two on the 3^{d} of May only—to spend all the 4th with my awful dentist again—arrived utterly spent & done & *dead*, with having travelled from California,[2] & (through it,) in a *madness* of brevity of time. I was *gone* & I cld. do nothing but tumble back here on the 5th, as I haven't, hadn't, been in N.Y. but for a couple of winter blizzards at all. And I am *still* dead, with that Western rush—I can't write as I ought. I can only love you & beg to be patient with me till about June 10th. *Then* I come back to you to lie at your feet, I sail July 4th.[3] Ever your affectionate

Henry James

NOTES

1 The date is written at the end of the letter.

2 James is referring to the journey that took him south and west, to California, giving lectures, the result being *The American Scene.*

3 James sailed back on the *Ivernia*, where Miss Robins was also a passenger. She apparently talked with James about a project for a novel called *The Chasm* (Robins pp 256–57).

LXXXIII

(Ms I S G M)

Lamb House, Rye, Sussex. July 30th 1906.[1]

Dearest Isabella Gardner!
I delight in this news of your near presence[2] & shall be delighted to see you here; though if you can't come I will come up to town to see you, unfailingly, & will there cherish & serve you to the utmost. Only make me the sign of your advent. Don't you remember being here seven (or whatever) years ago—on your way from Brussels[3]—just after I had settled here? It is the same humble home & still at your disposition. I enter into your abhorrence of travelling—without which I should be in Paris & at your feet. It has become *impossible*[4] to me, & I now languish in utter ignorance of foreign capitals & of the great movement of mankind; missing them, too, to make it worse, almost imperceptibly. Seriously, *do* (from London,) come down here for 24 hours. I will come up to town & fetch you. Give me therefore early notice & don't weary yourself meanwhile. I think with infinite pleasure of seeing you. Yours always & ever

Henry James

NOTES

1 The date is written at the end of the letter.

2 Mrs Gardner travelled to Europe, England, Italy and Paris, with Joseph Lindon Smith, who wanted to show her some of his art purchases for her, which were waiting for an export permit to be shipped to Boston.

3 November 1899; see letter 74.

4 James did travel again, going to the Continent in March–June 1907, stopping at Pau, and then to Paris (for nine weeks, visiting Edith Wharton), Rome (where Hendrik Andersen made a bust of him) and Venice; again in April–May 1908 to Paris; in 1910 to Bad Nauheim to join his brother William, and finally to the USA to accompany his brother, who died shortly after arriving (see letter 91, note 2).

LXXXIV

(Ms I S G M)

Lamb House, Rye, Sussex. August 10th *1906.*

My dear Isabella G.!
This is on the whole a sorry showing, as it throws me & my fond impatience off into a dim & indeterminate future & gives me no clue to your whereabouts[1] in the meantime. But I post myself on these shores all patiently & telescopically, & I watch for your advent with a vigilance that nothing shall foil. As for the season in which you are due here, there is bliss, after all, in counting on you to *égayer* the London autumn. And may your paths be pleasant, your pace reasonable & your concussions few in the meanwhile. But to this end get quickly out of the so deplorably *dismannered* & disqualified France. I am ever so obliged to you for being kind to earnestly-labouring (& I think really *endowed*—certainly with intelligence) Bill.[2] He wrote me of the pleasure he had had in breakfasting with you. I hope you turn your light & heat on Henry Adams,[3] from whom I have had too pensive or rather too

passionate, a letter—which I mean very soon to thank him for. And you *must* have treasures of anecdotes on the Minnie Pauls.[4] I count on these from you, & am devotedly yours

Henry James

NOTES

1 See letter 83.

2 William James, called 'Bill' or 'Billy', painter, one of the children of Henry's brother William, who was studying painting at the Académie Julien, in Paris, where he saw Mrs Gardner (see letter 85). He also went to Amsterdam. In March 1911 Mrs Gardner commissioned a portrait of Henry James by Bill when James was in Cambridge. It is now in the Blue Room at Fenway Court.

3 Henry Adams was in Paris. He was writing *The Autobiography of Henry Adams*, that was privately published in 100 copies, in 1907.

4 Paul and Minnie Bourget.

LXXXV

(Ms I S G M)

Lamb House, Rye, Sussex. September 9th 1906[1]

Dear Isabella Gardner,

This is a scrap of a word to keep myself a little in your memory—you having been very much in mine since I received your last good note. It demanded practically no immediate acknowledgment, & I hated to appear to pursue you again, too punctually, with oppressive penmanship. At the same time I wanted to thank you for having looked up, or made a sign to, dear groping, painting Bill,[2] & been kind to him—Bill who arrives here from Holland & other places tomorrow. He will tell me of his Paris vision of you, & I will tell him that I sit here yearning for (among other things,) a London one. Meanwhile my thoughts & prayers & wonderments go with you—my wonderments perhaps most of all, for I yearn especially over the question of where you can have been spending *les grandes chaleurs*—& hoping it may have been in no worst place than Venice. Only I don't see you in Venice & not at the Barbaro, & it is all vague & mixed & anxious to me. I have passed this admirable summer almost wholly in my garden, & am still finding it the best place. I wish you were due here earlier—but what garden is worth your wink? I hope you have removed Henry Adams[3] from the white heat of Paris & I am all impatiently & affectionately yours

Henry James

NOTES

1 The date is written at the end of the letter.

2 See letter 84, note 2.

3 See letter 84. Mrs Gardner was in Paris in June, then went to Madrid, was back in Paris on 14th July, went to Tours and Dinard from 29th July to the beginning of August, and was back in Paris again on 8th August, staying on into September.

LXXXVI

(Ms I S G M)

Lamb House, Rye, Sussex. November 14th *1906*

Dear Isabella G.!
This is delightful news—& I will with pleasure come & lunch with you at young Mrs. Frank Higginson's[1] on Dec. 3^{d}. This will suit me very much, as I *must* be in London the 1st, for a purpose, &, intensely pressed with occupation here, can not, alas, stretch my time there very far. *Do* blessedly make your advent the 2^{d}, & "give" me, as it were, the day or two after. I have just had very genial news of you from my nephew Bill & I yearningly await you, with all that you'll have to tell me of your unquenchable spirit of adventure—under the unquenchable star of your fortune! May Paris be easy to you meanwhile. Tom Perry[2] isn't with me yet—he's in London, but comes presently for 4 or 5 days. But I count those that separate you from your very affectionate old friend

Henry James

NOTES

1 Mrs Frank Higginson: the wife of Frank Higginson, brother-in-law of Mrs George Higginson, née Elizabeth Hazard Barker, daughter of Henry James's aunt; see *Notebooks* p 335.

2 Thomas Sargent Perry (1845–1928), American scholar and writer, old friend of Henry James from the Newport days. He taught in Japan and in France. In 1874 he married American Impressionist painter Lilla Cabot (1848–1933). James wrote about him in his autobiography, *Notes of a Son and Brother.*

LXXXVII

(Ms I S G M)

Lamb House, Rye, Sussex. November 21st *1906*

Dear Isabella G.!
Bravo again for the 3d. My address in London is always *Reform Club, Pall Mall, S.W.* I have a permanent room there, looking out on Carlton Gardens, ever so handy & yet so quiet, for stays of moderate duration. Please thank Mrs. Higginson for me very kindly & say to her that she may count upon me for Monday third Dec. at 1.30. And I note 103 Sloane St. Let me count upon you, by all means, for the rest of the afternoon. We will go not only "somewhere" but everywhere,[1] & I am yours always constantly

Henry James

NOTE

1 On 3rd January 1907, James wrote to Ariana Curtis: "I saw Mrs Gardner (went up to see her) in town and was divided between finding her battered, depleted, disfigured, and finding how fond one is of her, always, for the perfect terms one is on with her, her admirable ease, temper and facilité à vivre. She struck me as what she literally was and now is—a little ancient, rusty 'caretaker' or doorkeeper taking a holiday on money carefully saved up!" (Tharp p 272).

LXXXVIII

(Ms I S G M)

Lamb House, Rye, Sussex. May 11th 1909.[1]

My dear Isabella Gardner—

I have put it off—yes, just gracelessly & clumsily, but with fine canny calculations too, the pleasure of telling you how intensely touched I lately was by your beautiful & generous letter. The moment was a worrying & frustrating one—at which it came, & a combination of physical indispositions & anxieties (now more or less on the wane,) rested on me with a heavy pressure. So I just waited till a better hour, which has come—in fairly decent form at least, & I am justified of my fond wisdom by seeing how sweet it is now, in these easier conditions, to be making you even this poor sign. It's adorable to be talking with you again—even though I've no very shining or many-coloured news to give you. I am at the end of a very long continuous stay in this homely & healthy corner—so that if I have had in fact a rather lame or impotent winter (in respect of vulgar grossness of animal vigour,) the fault doubtless is my own. It has left me a bit compromised as a correspondent, & in the field of action generally, & there are arrears which, after such a crisis, one never makes up; but the well of affection gushes as pure within me as in sunnier years—besides which I intend to be pretty well again. I go up to London in a day or two to fight it out there (for change & movement's sake,) as long as possible; though the beauty & small poetry of this green countryside in these days of the first riot of blossom & early colour make me feel rather a fool to dream of anything else. I think the last personal flash of light on your splendid presence came to me from poor Mrs. Curtis (after her return hither from her stiff American pilgrimage!)[2] she told me you had shown her the kindness of an angel, & her *émerveillement* before the Palace was everything you could have desired. She is making a gallant & not altogether unsuccessful struggle at the Barbaro—hangs on there still, & I think might hang for some time (the next few years,) if the problem of her solitude[3] could be solved. Not only *I* can't solve it, however, but I don't see quite who can (as a companion & prop & aid to life,) complicated as it is a little by the fact that the "social & moral tone" of the place—the house's—with all its rigours & discriminations & exclusions, doesn't strongly appeal to the little world about her. However, sad histories arrive at denouements after their own ways. I forget really when we—you & I—last communicated. I was

3 or 4 months in Italy in the spring & early summer of 2 years ago. Venice was as adorable as ever (I was at the Barbaro, with dear old Dan still working the gondoliers like 60;) but Rome & Florence all ghosts & ruins. Maud Story[4] tragic, pathetic, in utter poverty; the Peruzzi[5] house (in Florence) dishonoured, desolate, sinister, & Edith now all but on the straw: I never want to see either place again. But Venice, yes, if you'll come out & take me there. Sargent's Lord Wemys[6] this year is said to be of the 1st order, but I shan't see it for 2 or 3 days. Ah, how I believe in your youth & your tambourine! The sound of the latter stirs at this distance your fondest faithfullest old

Henry James

NOTES

1 The date is written sideways at the end of the letter.

2 Mrs Curtis went to America after the death of her husband in 1908, to settle inheritance questions, and she visited Fenway Court in Boston.

3 Painter Frank Latimer, son of one of Ariana's sisters, Mary Wormeley Latimer (1822–1904), eventually settled in the Palazzo Barbaro, where he lived during World War I.

4 Maud Broadwood (d 1922) married in 1883 Waldo Story (1855–1915), sculptor, son of William Wetmore Story (1819–95), American Bostonian sculptor who had moved to Rome. James

committed himself to writing his biography, with scarce enthusiasm, on request of the widow: James eventually reconstructed in *William Wetmore Story and his Friends* (1903) the world of his "precursors", the generation of American artists who had preceded him in Europe. Sargent painted her portrait in 1883; see Ormond-Kilmurray 2002 pp 105–06. In 1903 Waldo left Maud and their two daughters, after falling in love with American opera singer Bessie Abott; see Lawrence pp 9–10. See also James's letter of 13th April 1907 to Howard Sturgis: "Bindo P's suicide was a horror I had yet to learn" (Edel *Letters IV* p 442), and the letter of 13th September 1907, to Clare Benedict: " … a few days in Florence (sad and overdarkened for me by dismal and sinister Story tragedies and miseries and follies which I heed in a manner—suicide of Bindo Peruzzi, babble of distracted mother etc—to be confronted with and immersed in)" (ibid p 460).

5 Edith Marion Story (1844–1907), daughter of William Wetmore Story, married the Florentine nobleman Cosimo Peruzzi. Her son Bindo was dismissed from the Italian army on a charge of homosexuality and committed suicide in Florence in 1907. She broke off with her younger son Ridolfo. On James's relation with William Wetmore Story and his children, see Lawrence.

6 Sargent painted a portrait of the Earl of Wemyss and March in London (1908), to celebrate the earl's ninetieth birthday, and portraits of several other members of the family. The earl's portrait was exhibited at the Royal Academy in 1909; see Ormond-Kilmurray 2003 no 556.

LXXXIX

(Ms I S G M)

Lamb House, Rye, Sussex. August 27th *1909.*

Dearest Isabella Gardner!
I have it before me, yes, tonight, the gentle letter of some little time since, in which you instructed me, in subtle sympathy with a weakness (of my cumbrous constitution) which I had then a little drivellingly perhaps reported to you, that I was to commemorate that crisis by writing to you, on the spot, all about it—but quite most particularly that it didn't exist. Well, you see how I always obey you to the letter—save for the trifle of doing so at the minute prescribed. It *doesn't* exist, any more, the crisis, & if I have delayed this to state it to you, you see the emphasis & assurance that the interval has enabled me to gain. I am ever so much better, quite a different creature—from the time when I had to account to you for my long & uncanny silence by telling you of my afflicted months during which everything but the most compulsory play of the pen was too distressful & impossible. Those months & that

phase of affliction are past, thank goodness—& I have got better by no dreary process of lying up, or even of lying down, but by simply, under the most enlightened advice & authority, indulging in a good deal *more* free motion than for a good while before. I had maltreated my poor old heart, it appeared (for considerable time back,) by not calling upon it to frisk & frolic *enough*—& with that pleasant prescription of increased license & reduced *surveillance* I appear to be quite recovering my equilibrium & a decent elderly measure of well-being. Forgive these fatuous details—there's nothing, in general, that I loathe more than fond prattle & complacent egotism about one's "symptoms." But I told you the little tale first only to explain the state of inability I was in then to do the civil thing—& now I tell it to explain away, in a manner, the explanation. So all seems well that ends well, & I again, before turning in, this rather sultry night of our too waning summer, greet you affectionately, devotedly. We have had a harsh & inclement season, nothing but cold & wind & wet, but it seems inclined to relent a little before it quite leaves us, & today has had that exquisite distilled quality of English fine weather in those rare fractions or specimens of it that are handed about like prized nectarines or chiselled nuts. I spent a couple of months in London (May & June) after last communicating with you—& they quite agreed with me as long as I didn't dine out (a practice I have come utterly to loathe & have wholly abjured;) & then returned here to an almost unnaturally quiet summer—more void of visitors & relatives than any year since I have lived here. The quietness, it is true, has been broken in upon by a certain amount of motor-ravage (I mean motor invasions from afar,) but this, clearly, we shall have now to reckon with forever—unless it is superseded by the descent upon us of aeroplanes as with the buzz of monstrous mosquitoes; such as we can't kill with the old effective clap of our two hands. You doubtless are subject to the same sort & degree of aggression—unless you are barricaded in your palace-fortress all the while—which heaven grant for the sake of a world greedy of you that you mayn't be. In fact you must have been at your Greenhill Dower House (the general charm & palatial staircase of which I vividly remember;) since you will certainly have let the great house if you wanted to—for when did you ever *not* do anything you wanted? So I figure you as embowered & peached & peared & plummed & graped, to say nothing of smotheringly *fleurie*, there: & so the beautiful memory of those too few (& too crowded!) days I spent with you comes back to me. I go up to town in a few days to do 3 or 4 things & see 3 or 4 (transient) persons—I shall probably say good-bye to poor dear Mrs. Curtis withal, as she presently departs for Venice after a summer spent in England in that concatenation of visiting for which she has, at her age, so wondrous a faculty. She goes forth on a continuous tour of 2 months, from house to house, & doesn't shrink even from the dreariest—not knowing always that they *are* so. I am very sorry for the loneliness of her Barbaro life now—during the long winter. She tries to get house-companions, but she lives in Venice in such a high & dry way—with such a terror of the "vulgar"—that is of the only pleasant & amusing people there—that the companions are appalled, in advance, at the prospect of weeks of that superiority, & I am afraid that though always famished for society, she has really made a desert about her. She has kindly asked me to go back with her & spend the autumn; but the last time I was with them, 2 years ago, they made me feel that they discriminated so invidiously against anyone I might weakly wish to see, of my little *other* promiscuous acquaintance in Venice, that I felt I could never again face the irritation and the inconvenience of it. Poor dear Dan'l was worse than she, but she's a good second. Ralph & his wife I nowadays simply never see—but the fragrance of his frivolity & the flushed rose pink of his image seem always to reach me from afar. I saw dear Gilliard Lapsley[1] when he passed through London rapidly on his way to Davos for the summer, & found him as ever absolutely charming & delightful; also fortified & rested from his former low estate. I am to see him again when he returns in October to see his doctors, who are to decide where he is to winter. He desires

Egypt, but they may decide California again. I really believe that with another year he will be able to take up his Cambridge position again—they are keeping it for him. But good night, ever yours

Henry James

NOTE

1 Gaillard Lapsley; see letter 67. James here and in letter 100 wrote 'Gilliard', a spelling that corresponds to the pronunciation.

XC

(Ms I S G M)

Lamb House, Rye, Sussex. Jan: 2d: 1910[1]

My dear Isabella Gardner—
This is a very poor & belated little word! Still, it is a little word of affection & remembrance; & it not only carries you the assurance of my fond fidelity—it gives you better news of your poor compromised old friend's personal situation[2] (compromised only physically,—not alas, for the fun & the refreshment & the little thrill if it, morally or "socially"!) than when he was last obliged to write pleading his infirmities & his decay. His decay seems for the time to be a little arrested—his infirmities to let him off more easily than he could hope a year ago; & though he has had, & we all have had, a deuce of a dreary year of it (a whole twelvemonth of *uninterrupted* darkness & deluge,) we mean positively to insist—*I* do, at any rate, & shall really take the matter up—on some sort of decent & honourable amends from 1910. So I just waggle this friendly hand at you from my utterly damp corner—so I just remind you

that my clinging inward interest in you never fails or falters—to my attached eyes all across the sea. At any rate it must—your existence, your situation, must be so *interesting.* May this inscrutable coming year do everything to enrich & fortify & further beautify it, & may you never doubt of the stout affection & fidelity of your all-constant old

Henry James

NOTES

1 The date is written at the end of the letter.

2 James was very ill at the end of 1909 and early 1910, to the point that he had a nurse at Lamb House.

XCI

(Ms I S G M)

Lamb House, Rye, Sussex. July 28th *1910*

Dearest Isabella Gardner!
Yes, I am coming out to see you & to thank you for your beautiful letter—tenderness for tenderness; & will joyfully pay you as long a visit as you will keep me for. We sail for Quebec on Aug.12—by the Canad: Pacific Line, & in the Empress of Britain: I say "we" for my brother & sister-in-law are still with me—only he, alas, very gravely ill. They came out to my ministering angel,[1] 4 months ago, he then very unwell[2]—but while I, through infinite pain & frustration & difficulty, have at last got more or less on the way to recovery, he is very much less well, & I am having a great tension of anxiety & distress. It's a *heart* business—& complicated. We are nursing him along into such amendment, if possible, as that he shall be *able* to sail. Pray for us all—for these are distressful days, & I am but partly on my own feet yet. But we shall see it through & you will find me again your fondest faithfullest old neighbour

Henry James

NOTES

1 Harry, William's son, had come to England to take care of his uncle, arriving on 24th February 1910, after the novelist had collapsed on 21st January. James had no physical ailment, but a deep despair, as Edith Wharton wrote visiting him on 18th March. William and Alice left for England, alarmed by Harry's news, on 29th March (Lewis T J p 580).

2 William James died on 26th August 1910, shortly after arriving back in the USA. On 3rd July, in Geneva, William and Henry had received the news of their brother Robertson's death.

XCII

(Ms I S G M)

Chocorua, N.H.[1] *Sept. 3d : 1910*

Dearest Isabella Gardner!

Sitting in darkness though I thoroughly am—for my beloved brother's death cuts into me in the deepest way—I feel the tenderness of your beautiful letter & warmly thank you for it. Our journey home & the weeks preceding it & the days since our arrival have all been as a black nightmare, of which the darkness will long be over us. He suffered in a way that it was anguish to see—to see helplessly—& at last only yearned to go; but that only adds to the bitterness. And the tide of his noble intellectual life was at its highest—yet nothing availed. My sister-in-law & her children—such interesting, charming young people—cling together but the closer. So I mean to stay on this side of the sea as long as possible (I mean all winter & on into the spring—unless the unexpected prevents,) in order not to be far from them. We remain here, if the season is favourable, through this month & then I go to Cambridge with them—to stay till the New Year. I shall then have no distant opportunity to see you—& shall eagerly make the most of it. I thank heaven I am here for these months—that is that I did come & that I was in fact intimately *with* William for many, many weeks as not for long years before. But we shall *talk*, better than this, & I am your faithfullest old friend

Henry James

NOTES

1 The heading is handwritten, on writing paper with black edges, for the deaths of William and Robertson.

XCIII

(Ms I S G M)

95 Irving St. *Cambridge*[1] Jan. 4th 1911.

My dear Isabella Gardner.

Yes, I've been odiously silent again—but there has been a dire inevitability in it; & I feel that you will generously take that statement from me without more analysis or explanation. There are times when life is so difficult that one has to throw overboard part of the cargo to save the ship. I don't mean by this I have thrown *you* overboard, in whatever peril—but only that during the wild confusion of such sacrifices one sometimes doesn't know quite what one is doing or *has* done, or where one is at all. The truth of this lurid picture is at all events quite compatible with the fact that I've perpetually yearned to see you again, & have, these last days, waited a little to thank you for your noble note only because of my being at the mercy of particular & exceptional hindrances. These are now, to all appearances, at an end, & I reach faithfully & affectionately out to you. Is there any afternoon or evening hour (after about *3* p.m.) that I might pass with you anyhow or anywhere? I would go with you, or *for* you, or *to* you—anywhither short of the stake, the scaffold or the "reception.") If you will telephone me here (3904 L.) any definite possibility that you *can* kindly entertain for me I will rush at once to your service—& to my delight. I have no definite engagement except on Friday evening next 6*th* (when I dine with an old dining-club of my youth;) till Friday 13th—when I go to New York for 4 or 5 days (to return here afterwards.) I should like immensely to come & occupy that turret chamber (or tower-bower for 3 or 4 days,) but perhaps that had better be *after* N.Y. Meanwhile call me by telephone for any meeting or greeting on earth (not flavoured with Japs or Smiths,[2] frankly!!) & I shall be more than ever your all-devoted old

Henry James

NOTES

1 Handwritten, on black-edged paper: The date is written at the end of the letter.

2 Joseph Lindon Smith, see letter 55. The 'Jap' is Japanese writer and scholar Okakura Kakuzō, whom Mrs Gardner employed for the Museum in 1904; see Tharp p 255.

XCIV

(Ms I S G M)

95 Irving St[1] *Jan: 5: 1911*

Dear Isabella Gardner!
I will come to you on Monday next at 4 with all joy. I came in today (from visit to my doctor in town) to learn almost brokenheartedly that you had been here & I had missed you. But how I shall try to make it up! No—it's not true, meanwhile, that I am "only bad & not ill"; I am ill & bad both, & insist on the benefit with you of both conditions; one of which will give me your pity & the other your sympathy! I leave you to guess *which which!* Yours always & ever

Henry James

NOTE

1 Written by hand, on black-edged paper.

XCV

(Ms I S G M)

Tavern Club,
4 Boylston Place. *March 9th* [1911]

My telephone no. at Cambridge is *3904L.*[1]

Dear Isabella Gardner.
What shall I do—very kindly tell me—telephone me—if you can—toward seeing you somehow before the 15*th*. I have been helpless & captive all these last days, & on the said 15*th* I go again to New York. I have "sat" day after day to dear Bill[2] (I had no soon descended from the devastating dental chair than I mounted the model stand;) & though the admirable result (incomplete still) immensely justifies me, the hole made in my time by such large allowances of it have made other activities so difficult as almost to be impossible—both the great added complication of social pursuits--& pursuit—in Boston on the basis of a domicile in Cambridge. And now I soon go away for a month[3]—& I greatly yearn to see you.[4] I dine out on Monday 13*th* & some people

come to us on Saturday—but tomorrow after sitting time, & on Saturday afternoon, & on Sunday after luncheon (till far into the night) & on Tuesday ditto I am *free*. Should I find you anywhere then, anywhere, anyhow? I knock at your door with this even now (this afternoon,) but despair of finding you; & launch thus the appeal of your much hampered but ever all faithful

Henry James

NOTES

1 The sentence with the telephone number is added by hand, while the letterhead is that of a Boston Club, which held concerts, using a piano given by Mrs Gardner.

2 For Bill James. The portrait was commissioned by Mrs Gardner, and James sat for it from 4th to 14th March. See *Notebooks* pp 332–33. See also letter 84, note 2.

3 James went to New York, where he saw Dr Joseph Collins for his health, sat for a portrait made by Cecilia Beaux, and did other errands; see *Notebooks* pp 332–33. See letter 97, note 3 for Cecilia Beaux.

4 James went to see Mrs Gardner on Friday, 11th March, "Dined Mrs Gardner and opera"; *Notebooks* p 332.

XCVI

(Ms I·S G M)

[March 1911]

I am in my bath!

Dear Mrs. Gardner.
A single word in great haste to say that I shall be delighted to come on Tuesday at 5. & to go with you on *Wednesday* evening. Very faithfully

H James

XCVII

(Ms I S G M)

Lowland House,
Nahant, P.O.,
Massachusetts.[1]

June 9th 1911.

Dear Isabella Gardner.
I rejoice then as to Monday next & thank you most kindly for so deciding the matter. I will be at Lynn Station, "fair or no fair" at 11.45 & bear you company to Gloucester.[2] It will be to *this* place I shall come back from Lynn in the p.m.—not to Cambridge (I stay on here some days longer;) but that is a detail & I easily get over from Lynn by the trolley-cars or a cab.—I don't quite understand whether *you* announce our appearance to Miss Baux,[3] (without the *e*,) *Green Alley, Gloucester, Mass*, or not; but I am at all events lucidly doing so by this very post—so all will be well. I hope you are ditto, & I pray daily for your ease & peace. This place does *me* good—it is superlatively fair. It is also superlatively still, with the murmur (or the roar) of the surf on the rocks the one most human sound. But

on Monday at ¼ to 12 we shall beat even that. Bon voyage! Yours all faithfully

Henry James

NOTES

1 The home of George Abbott James (b 1838), a dear friend of James's (not a relative), where he was a guest in the "torrid" summer of 1911. George James was a Ohio lawyer, who married Elizabeth Cabot Lodge in Boston in 1864.

2 Gloucester, on the Massachusetts coast. James went by train to Lynn Station, and then drove in a car with Mrs Gardner, to East Gloucester, to Cecilia Beaux's.

3 Cecilia Beaux (whose name James mostly got wrong) (1855–1942), a Philadelphia painter, who also studied in Paris at the Académie Julien. She became a well-known portrait painter and moved to New York in 1900, summering at Green Alley, Gloucester, where she lived the year round from 1906. Helena de Kay Gilder commissioned a portrait of Henry James from her in1911. James had posed for it in April (see letter 95, note 3) in Richard Watson Gilder's apartment, at 24 Gramercy Park; see *Cecilia Beaux Portrait* p 14 and *Notebooks* pp 329, 333–34.

XCVIII

(Ms I S G M, Lubbock)

Hill
Theydon Mount
Epping[1]

September 3^d 1911.

Telephone: 21 Epping.

Station & Telegraph Office.
Epping 3 miles

Dearest Isabella Gardner-
Yes, it has been abominable, my silence since I last heard from you—so kindly & beautifully & touchingly—during those few last flurried & worried days before I left America.[2] They were very difficult, they were very deadly days; I was ill with the heat & the tension & the trouble, &, amid all the things to be done for the wind-up of a year's stay, I allowed myself to defer the great pleasure of answering you, yet the great pain of taking leave of you, to some such supposedly calmer hour as this. "This," as it turns out, is but a repetition of the awful American condition, however—I mean condition of torrid air, & prolonged rain-famine & dried

up country; with others added, dismally—economic & labour convulsions, rumours of revolution & war, & consequent general depression & alarm: so that it hasn't been a "relief" to get home—it has rather been an aggravation, & I have been living not with renewed energy, but rather with renewed collapse, & hence haven't felt myself worthy to write. Take this belated expression therefore please not as the finally right & happy one, but only as a stopgap till a better is possible. I fled away from my little South coast habitation a very few days after reaching it—by reason of the brassy sky, the shadeless glare & the baked & barren earth, & took refuge among these supposedly dense shades—yet where also all summer no drop of rain has fallen. There is less of a glare nevertheless, & more of the cooling motor-car, & a very vast & beautiful old William & Mary (& older) house, of a very interesting & delightful character, which has lately come into possession of an admirable friend of mine Mrs. Charles Hunter, who tells me that she happily knows you & that you were very kind & helpful to her during a short visit she made a few (or several) years ago to America. It is a splendid old house—& though, in the midst of Epping Forest, it is but at ninety minutes' motor-run from London, it's as sequestered & woodlanded as if it were much deeper in the country. And there are innumerable other interesting old places about, & such old-world nooks & corners & felicities as make one feel (in the thick of revolutions) that anything that "happens"—happens disturbingly—to this wonderful little attaching old England, the ripest fruit of time, can only be a change for the worse. Even the North Shore[3] & its rich wild beauty fade by comparison—even East Gloucester & Cecilia's[4] clamorous little bower make a less exquisite harmony. Nevertheless I think tenderly even of that bustling desert now—such is the magic of fond association. George James's[5] shelter of me in his seaward fastness during those else insufferable weeks was a mercy I can never forget & my beautiful day with you from Lynn on & on, to the lovely climax above-mentioned, is a cherished treasure of memory. I water this last sweet withered flower in particular with tears of regret—that we mightn't have had more of them. I hope your month of August has gone gently & reasonably & that you have continued to be able to put it in by the sea. I found the salt breath of that element gave the only savour—or the main one—that my consciousness knew at those bad times; & if you cultivated it duly, & cultivated sweet peace, into the bargain, as hard as ever you could, I'll engage that you're better now—& will continue so if you'll only really take your unassailable *stand* on sweet peace. You will find in the depths of your admirable nature more genius & vocation for it than you have ever let yourself find out—& I hereby give you my blessing on your now splendid exploitation of that hitherto least attendend-to of your many gardens. Become rich in indifference—to almost everything but your fondly faithful old

Henry James

NOTES

1 The dwelling of Charles Hunter and Mary Smyth Hunter (1857–1933); Mary was a rich Maecenas of artists and painters, as well as a friend of James's. Sargent painted her portrait in 1898 (see Ormond-Kilmurray 2002 pp 150–51), and her daughters in 1900–02 (Ormond-Kilmurray 2003 pp 62–64), and Mrs Hunter again in 1902 (ibid p 93). Her sister was the musician and suffragette Ethel Smyth. Mary Hunter also rented Palazzo Barbaro in Venice and invited Claude Monet and his wife to stay with her in 1908. Monet painted the sketches for his famous series of Venice paintings, finished at Giverny, during this trip, which continued in a hotel after the Hunters left; see McCauley *Gondola Days* pp 240–43.

2 James had sailed back to England on 30th July, on the *Mauretania.*

3 The magnificent coast of Massachusetts, where Beverly was.

4 Cecilia Beaux; see letter 97.

5 See letter 97.

XCIX

(Ms I S G M)

Lamb House, Rye, Sussex. *October 24th* 1911.

Dear Isabella Gardner.

This is just to tell you that my joy in the statement of your good note, just received, as to your being bravely & beautifully well again is a kind of unutterable & immeasurable thing—without which you should have the full figure & pattern of it here. I get up to dance about for it, & I wish you could see me in the act—before I cut it short by reason of the extreme consequent vibrations of my sympathetic old house. I talked of you in this convinced sense with the poor dear much-wandering Sam Abbott[1] the other night, whom I met at dinner with Alice Mason & from whom I extracted every detail (of your current history,) that they could articulate. Mrs. Mason is much stricken, but you are on the rebound—that is what, that *was* what, remains with me; & even with this, I hasten to add, Alice M. is distinctly less enfeebled than she was—a year or two ago; & dispensed a most graceful hospitality, one feature of which was the exhibition of the 4 charcoal drawings lately done by Sargent (at the mere behest of her waved white hand) of her 2 nephews & 2 nieces,[2] admirably vivid Sargentesque heads & each done (which in the case of the 2 life-sized young soldiers was marvellous) in a single sitting. That ineffable genius has never, I think, done braver work than of late. I "settled in" here, as my neighbours call it, for the winter (more or less,) 3 weeks ago, but after a little found it wouldn't do at all & that the thrill of life & the fury of motion are (at the end of many years of rural hibernation) what I most want now. I fled up to London & shall practically winter there—only coming down here occasionally for a few days (as now) to hypnotize my forsaken servants into resignation with this inanity. You call me "mysterious"—but I find the concentrated contemplation of my mystery in solitude doesn't see *me*, at least, any further with it; I don't get to the bottom of it myself-& in town I am much more relieved from the futile effort to do so. I think fondly & gratefully of all your kindness to me last winter—the worrying through which (not the kindness but the winter,) whether in Cambridge, in Boston or in New York was, I may now confide to you, the toughest job I have *ever* had to tackle. Yet flowers sprouted in the grey *steppe;* those evenings at your board & in your box, those teatimes in your pictured halls, flush again in my mind's eye as real life-saving stations. It was even much of a reprieve from death to go with you that summer's day to lunch with the all-but deadly Cecilia; under the mere ghostly echo of the *énervement* of whose tongue I kind of wriggle & thresh about still—till rescued by the bounty of the dear young man, the Newfoundland-dog, the great St. Bernard nosing-in-the-snow-neighbour, of whose conveyance of me to his adjacent miraculous house, inanimate even though exasperated, I retain, please tell him, the liveliest, literally the fondest, appreciation.[3] Stranger even than some of the gods, in the great country, seemed to me some of the goddesses! However, it all makes for rosy romance—in snatches & patches now. An autumn gale is blowing & spattering about me here as I write & the wind sounds like great guns in my old chimneys. But my lawn is as lustrous as your finest emerald[4]—the one you wear on your left shoulder—or is it elbow, or knee?—& I have just been out to look at the private chrysanthemum show in my greenhouse—sighing with baffled pride that it can't be public. However, it doubtless creeps but painfully after your hundredth similar. But pressing labours—not in the outer, only in the innermost garden—sound their stern tocsin for me. The great thing for *you*, meanwhile, is to get exactly well enough, in your doctors' view, to be *able*, yet far from well enough not to *require*, to undertake that improving voyage to Europe which will involve a charitable sight of your all-fondly-faithful old friend

Henry James

NOTES

1 Samuel Appleton Browne Abbott (1846–1931), was a lawyer of an illustrious Boston family, and a highly-cultured and widely-read person. He graduated from Harvard in 1866, practised law from to 1868 to 1895, became a trustee and then President (1888–95) of the Board of Trustees of the Boston Public Library. He was essential in supporting the building and decorating of the McKim-Mead Building for the Library, but resigned after he was criticized in the papers for allowing Sargent to throw a party in the Library after completing his work there. He went to Italy and directed the American Academy from 1897 to 1903. He married three times, the last time in Rome, where he lived in the 'Villa Lontana', on the Via Cassia, receiving cardinals and ambassadors, as *The New York Times* reported (16th December 1911). I am grateful to Trevor Fairbrother for helping me to identify Samuel Abbott, and to Erica Hirschler for sending me material about him.

2 For Alice Mason, see letter 32. The four charcoals, all signed and dated 1911, are of the Balfours of Balbirnie, Alice Mason's grandchildren. Her daughter Isabella (1859–1938) had married Edward Balfour (1849–1927). The four are: Alice (b 1880); Eva (b 1888), married Sir Thomas Buxton, 5th Baronet; Edward William Sturgis (1884–1955), then a lieutenant in the British army, later a brigadier; and Robert Frederick (1883–1914), killed at Ypres. I owe these identifications to Richard Ormond, to whom I am extremely grateful. See also McKibbin p 82.

3 The episode has not been identified. Cecilia Beaux writes of the lunch with James and Mrs Gardner in her memoirs, with no

allusion to dogs or neighbours: "One day, during a brief visit of Henry James to this country, he came to lunch with me, in company with Mrs Gardner. It was a day of wet fog which he persisted in admiring, having found everything in America too hard and noisy … unendurable, in fact" (*Cecilia Beaux: Portrait of an Artist* p 233).

4 James is alluding to Mrs Gardner's passion for jewels. She had wonderful diamonds, 'The Rajah' and 'The Light of India', which she wore in her hair on springs (Carter p 56); she bought an exceptional ruby from Boucheron (p 127) and her rubies are visible in Sargent's portrait.

C

(Ms I S G M)

21 Carlyle Mansions
Cheyne Walk
S.W.[1] April 20*th* *1914.*

Dearest old friend!

I am more touched than I can say by your gentle & generous little words about my poor old *Notes*[2] & your report of Mrs. Fields's consecration[3]—which is what it really comes to—of my far-off impression of Dickens.[4] She knows, she *knew*, & what you quote from her gives me the greatest pleasure & a beautiful belated assurance. I like to have been *right* by such a co-operation of graceful & tender hands; it is, in the happiest way, something to go on with—till something more turns up! So kindly thank the venerable Priestess of that temple of Memories in Charles St.,[5] when you next have an opportunity, for having let me hang my offering there. Apropos of such matters, I cherish without the loss of a single shade of vividness my last fond vision of yourself. I question hard every chance witness who comes near me here & they all agree that you seem magnificent in your courage cheer & temper. Grandly flows on all this evidence, your current of life & strength. I nurse mine too along in spite of everything, & so we go on together. Much good may it do you to know it—yet any sign from *you* does *me* good. So there may be something in it; it can't *hurt* you at least to know that I yearn over you! I feel sure always that you are fighting the good fight—it refreshes and uplifts my spirit to see you *shine*, afar off, in your great position. A wandering gleam of the radiance reaches & makes brighter my own dusky little situation. I am as usual putting in the winter here (where in normal conditions I find it highly advantageous & hygienic;) but planning to go up to town for 3 or 4 months about March 1st. I change, you see, but from the blue bed to the brown, &, thank, the Lord, haven't an adventure to tell you of. Dear Gilliard Lapsley[6] spent 3 days with me just before he left for Egypt by the doctors' decree—& I have heard from him since at Assouan on the Upper Nile, where he will bore himself to death (he absolutely requires people like you & me;) but where I devoutly trust he will have put his last term of exile & be able to return to Cambridge & to Trinity, where he is highly prized & much held in affection. *I* hold him in it greatly—he is a gallant, delightful, quite heroic being; & I never forget that I originally owed my knowing him to a blest introduction of yours. I don't presume to ask you for your own news—*your* life being a dense splendid tissue of adventure—in fact *that* exactly it is that coruscates. You shine out to me with undiminished interest & in your splendid setting- of so much art & so much honour—&

I am your faithfullest, & from further back now surely than any one, old

Henry James

NOTES

1 This is James's address of the new place which he rented in October 1912, quite close to Emily Sargent's place.

2 *Notes of a Son and Brother* (1914), the second volume of James's unfinished autobiography, begun with *A Small Boy and Others* (1911), and continued, but not completed, with *The Middle Years.*

3 Annie Fields must have commented positively on a passage in James's autobiography where he recreated, using his father's letters, the atmosphere of older Boston, where the Fieldses' house was illuminated by "the light of literature", in a ray that descended "from a nearer heaven" (*Autobiography* pp 385–66). See letter 70, note 3.

4 James loved Dickens, and wrote about *Our Mutual Friend* in 1865; he remembered the indelible impression he had received, having seen Dickens during his visit to America in 1867, in *Notes of a Son and Brother* (*Autobiography* p 388). On Dickens and James, see Follini 2004.

5 The central street in Beacon Hill, the heart of Boston, still a most elegant area.

6 See letter 67.

BIBLIOGRAPHY

Works cited:

Adams *Novels*
Henry Adams *Novels, Mont Saint Michel and Chartres, The Education of Henry Adams, Poems* New York The Library of America 1983.

American Scene
Henry James *The American Scene* edited by Leon Edel Bloomington Indiana University Press 1968.

Anesko
Michael Anesko *Letters, Fictions, Lives, Henry James and William Dean Howells* New York Oxford University Press 1997.

Autobiography
Henry James *Autobiography* edited by Frederick Dupee Princeton Princeton University Press 1956.

Before Peggy Guggenheim
Before Peggy Guggenheim, American Women Art Collectors edited by Rosella Mamoli Zorzi Venezia Marsilio 2001.

Beloved Boy
Henry James *Beloved Boy, Letters to Hendrik C Andersen, 1899–1915* edited by Rosella Mamoli Zorzi Introductions by Millicent Bell and Rosella Mamoli Zorzi with an Afterword by Elena di Majo Charlottesville University of Virginia Press 2004.

Blanchard
Mary Warner Blanchard *Oscar Wilde's America* New Haven Yale University Press 1998.

Bourget
Paul Bourget *Outre-Mer (Notes sur l'Amérique)* Paris Alphonse Lemerre 2 vols 1895.

Cagidemetrio
Alide Cagidemetrio Introduction to *The Golden Bowl* New Milford, CT The Toby Press 2004 pp vii–xxxi.

Carter
Morris Carter *Isabella Stewart Gardner and Fenway Court* Boston The Isabella Stewart Gardner Museum 1972.

Cecilia Beaux Portrait
Cecilia Beaux: Portrait of an Artist An exhibition organized by the Pennsylvania Academy of the Fine Arts, 1974–75 Catalogue by Frank H Goodyear and Elizabeth Bailey Washington Museum Press 1974.

Chapman
John Jay Chapman *Memories and Milestones* New York Moffat, Yard & Co 1915.

Chong *Gondola Days*
Alan Chong *Artistic Life in Venice* in *Gondola Days. Isabella Stewart Gardner and the Palazzo Barbaro Circle* edited by Alan Chong, Richard Lingner, Elizabeth Anne McCauley, Rosella Mamoli Zorzi The Isabella Stewart Gardner Museum Boston Distributed by Antique Collectors' Club 2004 pp 87–128.

Curtis Viganò *Gondola Days*
Patricia Curtis Viganò *My Barbaro* in *Gondola Days* pp 203–13.

The Complete Letters
The Complete Letters of Henry James 1815–1872 edited by Pierre A Walker and Greg W Zacharias Introduction by Alfred Habegger Lincoln University of Nebraska Press vols I–II 2006

The Correspondence of William James, William and Henry edited by Ignas K Skrupselis and Elizabeth M Berkeley Charlottesville University Press of Virginia 4 vols 1993 …

Dearly Beloved Friends
Dearly Beloved Friends, Henry James's Letters to Younger Men edited by Susan E Gunter and Steven H Jobe Ann Arbor University of Michigan Press 2001.

Dear Munificent Friends
Dear Munificent Friends, Henry James's Letters to Four Women edited by Susan E Gunter Ann Arbor University of Michigan Press 1999.

Denker
Eric Denker *Whistler and Sargent circa 1880* in *Whistler and his Circle in Venice* London Merrell 2003 pp 23–33.

Edel *Complete Plays*
Henry James *The Complete Plays* edited by Leon Edel Philadelphia Lippincott 1949.

Edel *Conquest of London*
Leon Edel *The Conquest of London* Philadelphia Lippincott 1962.

Edel *Diary of Alice James*
The Diary of Henry James edited by Leon Edel Harmondsworth Penguin 1964.

Edel *Letters II* Edel *Letters III* Edel *Letters IV*
Henry James *Letters* edited by Leon Edel Cambridge The Belknap Press of Harvard University Press 4 vols 1974–84.

Ellmann
Richard Ellmann *Oscar Wilde* New York Knopf 1988.

Eye of the Beholder
The Eye of the Beholder, Masterpieces from the Isabella Stewart Gardner Collection edited by Alan Chong, Richard Lingner, Carl Zahn Boston The Isabella Stewart Gardner Museum in association with Beacon Press 2003.

Follini 2004
Tamara Follini *James, Dickens, and the Indirections of Influence* in *The Henry James Review* vol 25 No 3 Fall 2004 pp 228–38.

Francescato
Francescato, Simone *Collecting and Appreciating: Henry James and the Transformation of Aesthetics in the Age of Consumption* PhD Dissertation University of Venice Ca' Foscari 2007.

Freedman
Jonathan Freedman *Professions of Taste, Henry James, British Aestheticism and Commodity Culture* Stanford Stanford University Press 1990.

Goldfarb
Hilliard T Goldfarb *The Isabella Stewart Gardner Museum, A Companion Guide and History* The Isabella Stewart Gardner Museum Yale University Press 1995.

Hadley 1987
The Letters of Bernard Berenson and Isabella Stewart Gardner, 1887–1924,

with Correspondence by Mary Berenson edited by Rollin van N Hadley Boston Northeastern University Press 1987.

Horne
Henry James, A Life in Letters edited by Philip Horne London Allen Lane 1999.

Isabella Stewart Gardner e il suo mondo
'Gondola Days', Isabella Stewart Gardner e il suo mondo a Palazzo Barbaro-Curtis edited by Rosella Mamoli Zorzi Marano Edizioni della Laguna 2004.

Izzo
Henry James against the Aesthetic Movement edited by David Carrett Izzo and Daniel T O'Hara Jefferson, NC McFarland and Co 2006.

Kilmurray-Ormond
Sargent edited by Elaine Kilmurray, Richard Ormond Tate Gallery Publishing 1998.

Kossman
Rudolph R Kossman *Henry James: Dramatist* Groningen Wolters-Nordhoff 1969.

Lawrence
Kathleen Lawrence *Tragedies upon Tragedies.* Henry James and the Downfall of William Wetmore Story in *Ateneo Veneto* cxciv 6/11 2007 pp 1–20.

Letters from the Palazzo Barbaro
Henry James *Letters from the Palazzo Barbaro* edited by Rosella Mamoli Zorzi London Pushkin Press 1998.

Letters of Henry Adams
The Letters of Henry Adams edited by J C Levenson, Ernest Samuels, Charles Vandersee and Viola Hopkins Winner Cambridge The Belknap Press of Harvard University Press 3 vols 1982.

Letters of Mrs Henry Adams
Letters of Mrs Henry Adams, 1865–82 edited by Thoron Ward London Longmans, Green, and Co 1937.

Letters to Miss Allen
Lettere a Miss Allen, Letters to Miss Allen edited by Rosella Mamoli Zorzi Milano Archinto 1993.

Lewis
R W B Lewis *Edith Wharton, A Biography* New York Fromm 1985.

Lewis T J
R W Lewis *The James Family* London André Deutsch 1991

Lubbock
The Letters of Henry James edited by Percy Lubbock London Scribner's 2 vols 1920.

McCauley *Gondola Days*
Elizabeth Anne McCauley, *A Sentimental Traveler: Isabella Stewart Gardner in Venice* in *Gondola Days* cit pp 3–52.

McKibbin
David McKibbin *Sargent's Boston* Boston The Museum of Fine Arts 1956.

Mamoli Zorzi 1999
Rosella Mamoli Zorzi *The Pastimes of Culture, The tableaux vivants of the British Expatriated in Venice in the 1880s and 1890s* in *Textus* xii no 1 pp 77–95.

Mamoli Zorzi 2002
Rosella Mamoli Zorzi *Art in the museums and art in the homes, Tableaux Vivants in Isabella Stewart Gardner's Time* in *Annali di Ca' Foscari* 41 2002 pp 63–89.

Monteiro
George Monteiro *Henry James and John Hay, The Record of a Friendship* Providence Brown University Press 1965.

Notebooks
The Complete Notebooks of Henry James edited by Leon Edel and Lyall H Powers Oxford University Press 1987.

Ormond-Kilmurray *The Early Portraits*
Sargent, The Complete Works, The Early Portraits edited by Richard Ormond and Elaine Kilmurray New Haven Yale University Press 1998.

Ormond-Kilmurray 2002
Sargent, The Complete Works, The Portraits of the 1890s edited by Richard Ormond and Elaine Kilmurray New Haven Yale University Press 2002.

Ormond-Kilmurray 2003
Sargent, The Complete Works, The Later Portraits edited by Richard Ormond and Elaine Kilmurray New Haven Yale University Press 2003.

Painter's Eye
Henry James *The Painter's Eye* edited by John L Sweeney

Foreword by Susan M Griffin Madison University of Wisconsin Press 1989.

Perosa
Sergio Perosa Henry James and the Unholy Art of Acquisitions in *The Cambridge Quarterly* 2008 pp 150–63.

Perry
Virginia Harlow *Thomas Sargeant Perry: A Biography and Letters to Perry from William, Henry, and Garth Wilkinson* Durham, NC Duke University Press 1950.

Powers 1990
Henry James and Edith Wharton *Letters 1900–1915* edited by Lyall H Powers London Weidenfeld and Nicolson 1990.

Prefaces
Henry James *Literary Criticism* edited by Leon Edel New York Library of America 2 vols 1984.

Robins
Elizabeth Robins *Theatre and Friendship, Some Henry James Letters with a Commentary* London Jonathan Cape 1932.

Roman
Judith A Roman *Annie Adams Fields, The Spirit of Charles Street* Bloomington Indiana University Press 1990.

Sargent's Venice
Sargent's Venice edited by Warren Adelson, William H Gerdts, Elaine Kilmurray, Rosella Mamoli Zorzi, Richard Ormond, Elizabeth Oustinoff New Haven Yale University Press 2006.

Scenic Art
Henry James *The Scenic Art, Notes on Acting and the Drama: 1872–1901* edited by Allan Wade New Brunswick Rutgers University Press 1948.

Selected Letters
Henry James *Selected Letters* edited by Leon Edel The Belknap Press of Harvard University Press 1987.

Shand-Tucci
Douglas Shand-Tucci *The Art of Scandal, The Life and Times of Isabella Stewart Gardner* New York Harper Perennial 1997.

Spongberg
Stephen A Spongberg *Exploration and Introduction of Ornamental and Landscape Plants from Eastern Asia* in J Janick and J E Simon eds. *New Crops* New York Wiley 1993 pp 140–47.

Strouse
Jean Strouse *Alice James* London Jonathan Cape 1981.

Tharp
Louise Hall Tharp *Mrs Jack, A Biography of Isabella Stewart Gardner* New York Congdon and Weed 1965.

Tintner
Adeline Tintner *The Museum World of Henry James* Ann Arbor, Michigan UMI Research Press 1986.

Tintner 1993
Henry James and the Lust of the Eyes Baton Rouge Louisiana University Press 1993.

Whistler
The Correspondence of James McNeil Whistler University of Glasgow website.

Wrenn
Angus Wrenn *Henry James and the Second Empire* London Legenda 2009.

Other Sources

Letters by Henry James

Beloved Boy, Letters to Hendrik C Andersen, 1899–1915, Introductions by Millicent Bell and Rosella Mamoli Zorzi with an Afterword by Elena di Majo Charlottesville University of Virginia Press 2004.

Dearly Beloved Friends, Henry James's Letters to Younger Men edited by Susan E Gunter and Steven H Jobe Ann Arbor University of Michigan Press 2001.

Dear Munificent Friends: Henry James's Letters to Four Women edited by Susan Gunter Ann Arbor University of Michigan Press 1999.

Henry James, A Life in Letters edited by Philip Horne London Allen Lane 1999.

Henry James and John Hay, The Record of a Friendship edited by George Monteiro Providence Brown University Press 1965.

Lettere a Miss Allen, Letters to Miss Allen edited by Rosella Mamoli Zorzi Milano Archinto 1993.

Letters edited by Leon Edel Cambridge The Belknap Press of Harvard University Press 4 vols 1974–84.

Letters from the Palazzo Barbaro London Pushkin Press 1998.

The Complete Letters of Henry James 1855–1872 edited by Pierre A Walker and Greg W Zacharias Introduction by Alfred Habegger Lincoln University of Nebraska Press vols I–II 2006 …

The Complete Letters of Henry James 1872–1876 edited by Pierre A Walker and Greg W Zacharias Introduction Millicent Bell vol I 2008

The Letters of Henry James edited by Percy Lubbock London Scribner's 2 vols 1920.

Other collections of letters

Henry James and Edith Wharton: Letters, 1900–1915 edited by Lyall L Powers London Weidenfeld and Nicolson 1990.

Henry James's Waistcoat, Letters to Mrs Ford, 1907–15 edited by Rosalind Bleach Foreword by Philip Horne York Stone Through Books 2007.

The Correspondence of Henry James and Henry Adams, 1877–1914 edited by George Monteiro Baton Rouge Louisiana University Press 1992.

The Correspondence of William James, William and Henry 1897–1910 edited by Ignas K Skrupskelis and Elizabeth M Berkeley Charlottesville University Press of Virginia vol 3 1994.

The Death and Letters of Alice James edited by Ruth Bernard Yeazell Berkeley University of California Press 1981.

The Letters of Bernard Berenson and Isabella Stewart Gardner 1887–1924, with Correspondence by Mary Berenson edited by Rollin van N Hadley Boston Northeastern University Press 1987.

Thomas Sargeant Perry: A Biography and Letters to Perry from William, Henry, and Garth Wilkinson by Virginia Harlow Durham, NC Duke University Press 1950.

Theatre and Friendship, Some Henry James Letters with a Commentary by Elisabeth Robins London Jonathan Cape 1932.

Works by Henry James

Autobiography edited by Frederick Dupee Princeton Princeton University Press 1956.

Collected Travel Writings New York The Library of America 2 vols 1993.

Complete Tales of Henry James 12 vols edited by Leon Edel Philadelphia Lippincott 1962–64.

Henry James on Culture. Collected Essays on Politics and the American Social Scene edited by Pierre A Walker Lincoln University of Nebraska Press 1999.

Italian Hours edited by John Auchard University Park Pennsylvania Pennsylvania State University Press 1992

Literary Criticism edited by Leon Edel New York Library of America 2 vols 1984.

New York Edition New York Scribner's Sons 1907–09 New York Scribner's 24 vols 1971.

Novels 1871–80 edited by William T Stafford New York Library of America 1983.

Novels 1881–86 edited by William T Stafford New York Library of America 1985.

Novels 1886–90 edited by Mark Fogel New York Library of America 1989.

Novels 1896–99 edited by Myra Jehlen New York Library of America 2003.

Novels 1901–02 edited by Leo Bersani New York Library of America 2006.

The American Scene edited by Leon Edel Bloomington Indiana University Press 1968.

The Complete Notebooks of Henry James edited by Leon Edel and Lyall Powers New York Oxford University Press 1987.

The Complete Plays of Henry James edited by Leon Edel Philadelphia Lippincott 1949.

The Painter's Eye edited by John L Sweeney Madison University of Wisconsin Press 1989.

The Scenic Art, Notes on Acting and the Drama: 1872–1901 edited by Allan Wade New Brunswick Rutgers University Press 1948.

Biographies

Fred Kaplan *Henry James, The Imagination of Genius* New York William Morrow 1992.

Leon Edel *Henry James* Philadelphia Lippincott 5 vols 1953–72.

Leon Edel *Henry James, A Life* New York Harper and Row 1985.

Lyndall Gordon *A Private Life of Henry James, Two Women and His Art* London Chatto and Windus 1998.

Sheldon M Novick *Henry James, The Young Master* New York Random House 1996.

Sheldon M Novick *Henry James, The Mature Master* New York Random House 2007.

Bibliography

Leon Edel and Dan H Laurence *A Bibliography of Henry James* London Rupert Hart-Davis 1961.

On Isabella Stewart Gardner and the Museum:

Bellini and the East edited by Caroline Campbell and Alan Chong Boston The Isabella Stewart Gardner Museum 2005.

Cultural Leadership in America, Art Matronage and Patronage Boston Isabella Stewart Gardner Museum vol XXVII 1994.

The Eye of the Beholder, Masterpieces from the Isabella Stewart Gardner Museum edited by Alan Chong, Richard Lingner, Carl Zahn Boston The Isabella Stewart Gardner Museum in association with Beacon Press 2003.

Journeys East, Isabella Stewart Gardner and Asia Exhibition Catalogue edited by Alan Chong, Richard Lingner, Noriko Murae Pittsburgh Periscope Press 2009.

Goldfarb, Hilliard T *The Isabella Stewart Gardner Museum, A Companion Guide and History* The Isabella Stewart Gardner Museum Yale University Press 1995.

Gondola Days, Isabella Stewart Gardner and the Palazzo Barbaro Circle edited by Allan Chong, Richard Lingner, Elizabeth Anne McCauley, Rosella Mamoli Zorzi The Isabella Stewart

Gardner Museum Boston Distributed by Antique Collectors' Club 2004.

'Gondola Days'. Isabella Stewart Gardner e il suo mondo a Palazzo Barbaro-Curtis edited by Rosella Mamoli Zorzi Marano Edizioni della Laguna 2004.

The Letters of Bernard Berenson and Isabella Stewart Gardner 1887–1924, with Correspondence by Mary Berenson edited by Rollin van N Hadley Boston Northeastern University Press 1987.

Anne Hawley *Isabella Stewart Gardner, An Eye for Collecting* in *Before Peggy Guggenheim, American Women Art Collectors* edited by Rosella Mamoli Zorzi Venezia Marsilio 2001.

Kathleen D McCarthy *Isabella Stewart Gardner and Fenway Court* in *Women's Culture* Chicago University of Chicago Press 1991.

Louise Hall Tharp *Mrs Jack, A Biography of Isabella Stewart Gardner* New York Congdon and Weed 1965.

Aline B Saarinen *C'est mon plaisir* in *The Proud Possessors* London Weidenfeld Nicolson 1959.

Cynthia Saltzman *Old Masters, New Worlds, America's Raid on Europe's Great Pictures 1880—World War I* New York Viking 2008.

Antonella Trotta *Rinascimento americano, Bernard Berenson e la collezione Gardner, 1894–1924* Napoli La Città del Sole 2003.

General Bibliography

Bill Brown *A Sense of Things, The Object Matter in American Literature* Chicago University of Chicago Press 2003.

Colleen Denney *At the Temple of Art, The Grosvenor Gallery, 1877–90* Madison Farleigh Dickinson University Press 2000.

The Culture of Consumption: Critical Essays in American History 1880–1980 edited by R W Fox and Jackson Lears New York Pantheon 1893.

Thorstein Veblen *A Theory of the Leisure Class* edited by Martha Banta Oxford Classics 2007.

Other Manuscripts at the Isabella Stewart Gardner Museum

John L Gardner *Travel Diaries.*

Guestbook 1897–99.

Scrapbooks.

ACKNOWLEDGEMENTS

I would like to thank Anne Hawley, the Norma Jean Calderwood Director of the Isabella Stewart Gardner Museum in Boston, for the enthusiasm with which she has welcomed this and other projects connected with the museum, and also for allowing me to reproduce material belonging to the Isabella Stewart Gardner Museum; Alan Chong, Curator of the Isabella Stewart Gardner Collection, for agreeing to write his essay and for the generous help given to me on various occasions. I would also like to thank Richard Lingner, for graciously allowing me to check dates and places on his own Gardner calendar and for sending me useful suggestions and material; Mario Pereira and Kristin Parker for having made easier my work with the James manuscripts.

My gratitude continues towards the late Alexander R. James, who always encouraged me in my jamesian projects, and now towards his daughter, Bay James.

My deep gratitude to Tamara Follini, Clare College Cambridge; Philip Horne, University College London; Pierre Walker, Salem State College and editor of The Complete Letters of Henry

James *with Greg Zacharias; and my Jamesian friends and colleagues, for their generosity in helping me in many ways over the years.*

I would also like to thank Richard Ormond, editor of the catalogue raisonné of John S Sargent, The Complete Paintings, *Yale University Press, 1998 … , with Elaine Kilmurray, for his help in identifying some of Sargent's works cited by James. I am grateful to Trevor Fairbrother for helping me to identify a friend of James's and for other useful suggestions; to Werner Sollors of Harvard, for making it possible for me to use and enjoy the Harvard libraries over the years.*

My thanks to Elisabeth Fairman, Senior Curator of Manuscripts, and Naomi Saito, of the Beinecke Library, for sending me material; to Victoria Perry, of Hatfield House; to Simon Blundell, librarian, of The Reform Club; and to Tom Carter, of the Salem Philips Archives for providing answers to my queries.

ROSELLA MAMOLI ZORZI

PHOTOGRAPHIC CREDITS

p 8 *Mrs Gardner in Venice* 1894 Anders Zorn

p 26 *Beacon Street Drawing Room*

p 30 *Henry James's bed in the Palazzo Barbaro*

p 48 *Beacon Street Drawing Room*

p 114 *Isabella Stewart Gardner in Venice*

p 311 *View of the courtyard of Fenway Court* 1903

All images © Isabella Stewart Gardner Museum Boston